Joy, Arlin and Friends, Great Depression

White Trash

Redeemed

Life Edition

Joy Gartman

WHITE TRASH Redeemed Life Edition

Copyright © 2012 by Joy Gartman

All rights reserved. This book is protected by the copyright laws of the United States of America. This book may not be copied or reprinted for commercial gain or profit. The use of short quotations or occasional page copying for personal or group study is permitted and encouraged.

ISBN 978-1-60458-928-3

To contact the author, please email:
joygartman@gmail.com

Published 2012 by Instant Publishers

Endorsements

"*Your book made me cry. It caused me to open my closet, and it rattled my bones.*"

Billy, trailer park neighbor

Knocked down, but not knocked out!
The tenacity of the human spirit . . .
To know and be known,
To love and be loved;
A collision course between growing peril and self-destruction
But Destiny awaits . . . .
A breath-taking, yet sobering story of redemption from the lies we believe that imprison our soul and take captive our identity
This book gives victims a voice: a must-read for therapists, clinicians, pastors, lay persons from the perspective of an abused and exploited generation.

Gail McMackin, Pastoral Counselor
Redeeming Love prayer ministry
www.healingprayerministry.net

"*Touching, raw, beautifully honest...To anyone who has been through the school of hard knocks, there is hope!*"

Tracy, housewife, mother and grandmother

"*Great book, Joy! We're proud of you!*"

KiMar, daughter-in-law

"Hi Joy, I am very much enjoying your book, and I think in a lot of ways I can relate to you, that's why I enjoy reading it."

Rachael, 23 and under house arrest

"White Trash is a powerful reminder that the truth sets us all free. I am deeply inspired to seek my own truth and move forward because of this book."

Becky, mother, author of Cookingforafrica.com, and abuse survivor

"This little book delivers a punch for all of us who have lived through seeking peace from what this world offers, only to find confusion and more of the same. It has a drawing power to want more."

Beverly, retired teacher

"WHITE TRASH REDEEMED is a sober reality of the pain and hurts that come to people in this world. Joy has endured much. Yet, the bigger story of her life has been in receiving the faithful love of Jesus and His extraordinary compassion in bringing life, hope, and healing in the midst of brokenness. Joy's life story is a great faith builder, and her book is an excellent tool to be given away. It offers hope and encouragement to those in despair."

Bob Hasty, Co-Senior Pastor, The Rock of Roseville (CA)

Acknowledgements

KiMar and Molly, you are not only wonderful daughter-in-laws, you are wonderful editors. I appreciate you both for all your hard work. France, may God bless you for your time in editing and your encouraging words about writing.

Margaret and Kelly, the healings you both experienced are so incredible. Thanks for sharing so others may be blessed.

Great intercessors were vital to the writing of this book. Theresa McNabb, Joe and Rose Calabrese, Bev McNulty, Sherry Montna, Joanna and Brad Taylor thank you, thank you, thank you. Without your consistent prayers this book would not be all it was intended it to be.

Dedication

This book is dedicated to my children. Tracy Dumlao, Shaun, David and Dru Gartman—you have gone with me through the storm and through the mud. I am so grateful for each of you and love you more than you can possibly know.

Contents

Foreword i
Author's Preface iii

White Trash 1
Lessons from Mom 9
The Last Slap 13
Onions to Eat 17
From Frying Pan to Fire 21
A Heathen with God 25
Cinderella 27
Snow White 31
The Risk of Loving 35
Signs and Wonders 39
In Love but Rejected 45
I Had a Dream 49
Run for Your Life 53
Why These Parents? 57
On the Move 59
Wilderness Flowers 61
The Dixie Cup 71
Episcopal Priest: Isn't That a Hoot? 73
Round-Up of Children 75
Fires 79
Margaret's Testimony 83
Vision of Revival 91
Beauty for Ashes 95
Amazing Grace 103
Alone 111

Endnotes 119

Foreword

A bucket full of cherries and life full of pits...

Standing under Grandma's cherry tree, ominous and foreboding, I wondered how I was going to conquer it. It stood looking down on me, taunting me to break free from my earthbound perspective and take the risk it offered as it held out its best fruit. It challenged me to see everything from a new, yet risky, perspective. I can still hear the creak of the old picking ladder's frame as I watched it shudder all the way to the top. I knew the challenge before me was to take the first step.

Like facing the ominous cherry tree, writing a book about one's past is wrought with both internal and external challenges. It's packed with suppressed emotions and feelings as one risks his or her reputation in an attempt to find a balance between revealing the deep darkness of the pits and the beauty rising from the ashes that remain. The author takes the risk so that we, the readers, may find Faith, Hope and Love in the higher reaches her story...

My mom's story is just that...her journey is full...

Full of fate...
Full of pain...
Full of regret...
Full of redemption...
And, of course, full of Joy!!

Joy Gartman

Standing on the top of the ladder in the midst of the branches of the cherry tree, I believe I felt the same fear, intimidation, exhilaration and accomplishment that my mom has felt while writing her story. What I choose to keep in my heart about her adventure and mine is this...

Although the challenges were intense, the rewards are sweet and the view from above is amazing!

My Mom = My Hero

Shaun Gartman

Author's Preface

Why Am I Afraid to Tell You Who I Am? was a book written by John Powell in the late 1960s. The title of this classic book describes exactly the fear I had of writing a book detailing my life. Indeed, it was scary to allow the well-guarded, dark secrets of my life to come out in the open. It is hard to be that transparent, especially for those who, like me, have learned at an early age, "not to hang all the family's laundry out for everyone to see." First, there is the shame, and then there is the fear that, if I tell you who I really am, not only will you judge me, but you may also reject me or limit me. I will be found stripped of my on-public-display image, and if you don't like who I really am, I will have nothing left to offer.

I've heard that we are the sum total of our choices, and during my lifetime I've made a lot of lousy ones. Other people's choices also shape us. Past choices, circumstances, sins, and regrets taunted me as I wrote this book. What happened in my life has happened in so many lives, and my suffering may seem insignificant to some. Nonetheless, the pain of it was real, and the impact of that pain on my life was huge. Even worse, the fallout of my poor choices on my children's lives was very damaging. I pray that opening up my life will help heal my children and… maybe even help to bring just a little bit of healing into your life.

White Trash

I'm not sure why I was born white trash—I just was. I don't know why my parents became my parents. I don't know why a person is born where and when they are born. And I don't know why people are born different. As a child these thoughts never entered my mind. I did what children do. Whether we are born into love and riches or into desperation, we adapt to our conditions. But, without a doubt, we are shaped by what surrounds us. Our surroundings become our *normal* world, whether *normal* or not.

When I was born, my parents were facing the challenges caused by the Great Depression. Multitudes were looking for jobs, including my dad. Both of my parents had grown up on farms—Dad in West Virginia and Mom in Missouri—and they had known hard times, but nothing like what they went through at that time. They met and married in Oklahoma City, and my brother was born there. I was born in Middletown, Ohio, in 1941. By 1942, we were on the move looking for work. We were lucky. We owned a car and could travel to places where work was available.

The Great Depression started in 1929 with the fall of the stock market. It lasted all through the thirties and rippled into the forties. During the depression, there were times when almost half of all Americans were barely eking out a living. Forty percent of the banks failed and multitudes lost everything. Even the farms lost about half of their value. Those who had lost their savings and jobs found it hard to rebound. We were among those who struggled.

Farrel, my dad, was a plumber by trade, and most of the places that had his type of work were boom towns, oil towns, and the like. The jobs were temporary, but for the times the pay was good. Moving every few months would become our way of life for the next fourteen years. Usually the places where we landed were dusty. I don't remember green grass or trees, and the available housing often left much to be desired. Most of the places we lived in didn't have indoor plumbing, which meant we usually had outhouses and wells. One of the nicer houses that we lived in had an indoor hand pump in the kitchen. But it also had snakes under the back porch. Once we lived in a converted barn and another time in an old discarded box car, but Mom always cleaned and fixed things up the best she could. She usually made curtains, sometimes out of flour sacks. Some of my dresses were also made out of the cloth they used for flour sacks. They often had flowers on them. I liked the ones with flowers. She was a good seamstress and a great housekeeper.

Mom liked things clean and tidy. When we were young, she would do the wash outside in a wash tub. She would use a rubboard and some blue whitening stuff. She prided herself in sparkling white sheets hanging on the clothesline. She worked hard to make sure that everything was shiny and clean, even in such dirty conditions. Arlin and I also took our baths in the wash tub, and Mom wanted us clean.

White Trash

Arlin, my older brother, was nineteen months old and I was six months old when our family moved. With Arlin, they had already moved once before I was born. When everyone else you know is moving, it seems like the whole world is moving too. It was not until the fourth grade when I figured out that not everybody moved all the time. That same year I discovered that my middle name was Denean. My full name was Joy Denean Gatts, and my brother's name was Arlin Jay Gatts. Arlin was named after my mom, Arlene.

I liked it when we traveled, because we would eat out and sing. Mom had a good voice and Arlin did too. I would often sing quietly to myself as I looked out the window. I never felt like I sang as nicely as Arlin. For that matter, I didn't do anything as good as Arlin—except school. He was smarter, but I would work harder. It felt good to excel at something. Dad had a fourth grade education, and Mom had finished the eighth grade. Her goal for us was to complete high school. Even though I studied hard, English and spelling were hard for me. I was always embarrassed when I had to read out loud or stand up and join the spelling bees. It was only much later that they discovered I had dyslexia. Arlin didn't have to work as hard and did fairly well, especially considering all the moving we did. We never started and finished a school year in the same school until I was in the ninth grade.

Sometimes there weren't jobs at the construction sites, so Dad would work on farms or at whatever else was available. I remember carrying water for the adults while they were hoeing cotton and selling corn out of the back of a truck. Arlin and I helped my mom pick tomatoes to buy our school clothes when we were ten to twelve years old. It's amazing how normal this all seemed. There were other kids working with their parents, so I don't remember thinking of it as odd or out of the ordinary. If we wanted to play, there always seemed to be other kids around. When we were living in the boom towns, the children were white. If we were working on the farms in the South, the children would often be black. Their color never mattered to us; we just enjoyed our friends. I think children are colorblind unless someone teaches them otherwise.

One day, while we were in the South, a southern lady, her husband and her daughter rode out in a fancy car to where we were living. Her husband seemed to be in charge of the farm workers. He got out of the car and walked over a short distance to a group of the laborers, including my dad.

He left the ladies in the car. After a few minutes they got out of the hot car and began fanning themselves with fancy white fans. The lady had on a white flowing dress with little pink flowers and shiny pink ribbons that matched the flowers. I was admiring how beautiful she and her daughter were. Their dresses were similar, but not exactly the same. They were talking softly, but they were really close to where my brother and I had been playing. Now we were just standing there gawking. I couldn't hear what the younger girl said, but I can still hear what the lady said in response. Her voice was as sweet as I had ever heard. They were looking straight at my brother and me when she cooed with her beautiful southern drawl, "Sweetie, they're just poor *white trash.*"

Before that I had never thought about what or who I was. But now I knew. I was *trash*. Perhaps all the poor white folk who worked in the fields were considered white trash. But as a child, I didn't know what white trash meant, I just knew that it wasn't good. I knew that we were not as good as they were—those people who made more money or people who were more educated. That was my first sting of rejection from the world outside my family. That label helped me form an opinion of myself and my family—and not a good one. No matter what I did, that label stuck in my mind.

Even now I'm not sure what white trash really means. It means different things to different people. But as a child, it meant everything that was wrong with our family. We were uneducated, poor, and we were bad.

I didn't know anything about the term *sexual abuse* when I was a child, but I knew that what was happening to me made me bad. And this *badness* had been going on for quite a while. At first it was my uncle when I was about four, then my dad a year or so later. After I became an adult, I discovered that my dad's brother, Uncle Wilbur, was in fact my father. Fortunately, we moved away from Uncle Wilbur before anything got beyond the fondling stage. With Dad, it was different. There were touches and cuddles and tucking into bed. He moved slowly at first. Gradually, it became more and more until it was full-blown incest.

Deep inside of me, I knew it was wrong, and I felt shame. For some reason, I even felt it was my fault—maybe because when I would go to Mom, she wouldn't believe me. That really hurt because I had hoped that she would defend me. I was taught young to bury my hurts and my feelings because it just hurt more if my feelings were exposed, and then ignored or rejected.

Alcohol was common in our home. Mom and Dad consumed a lot of Jack Daniels, especially on weekends. Mom had a real temper and a quick back-of-the-hand to my face and more so if she had been drinking. I learned to say, "Yes ma'am" and never to talk back or question what I was told. We knew that children were to be seen and not heard. Mom would sometimes entertain gentlemen friends when Dad wasn't around. Mom and Dad were separated many times, but Mom would always go back to him, maybe because she couldn't make ends meet.

One time when I was about four and Dad was gone, Mom sent me outside. After a while, I got thirsty and went into the house to get a drink from the water pitcher on the kitchen counter. When Mom heard me, she came rushing into the kitchen, hopping mad. I darted out the back door, but she picked up a butcher knife and started after me. Then she chased me around the backyard with the butcher knife. She probably just wanted to scare me. Well, she sure did.

When I was an adult, Mom told me that when I was born, Arlin was only thirteen months old and still nursing, so Mom continued nursing him and gave me a bottle propped on a pillow. She said that I was a "good" baby. But later, I started rocking back and forth as I sat on the couch. This embarrassed and angered my mom. I remember her putting me in the attic to try to scare me into stopping. It didn't work. The rocking continued. I also fidgeted a lot, and this irritated her even more. She would often slap me, but that didn't work either. I would soon forget and fidget again. Once in awhile, when she told me to quit, I would do it just one more time as an act of defiance. Sometimes she would slap me, but sometimes I would get by without getting slapped. I don't remember ever going against her in any other way, and I don't know why I challenged her in this way, especially knowing that I might get slapped.

Lessons from Mom

When I was in high school, my mom taught me to steal. In a weird way, this was a bonding time for Mom and me. She reasoned that others were rich, and we were poor. She said, "They won't even miss it." She also told me that because I was a minor, I wouldn't get jailed. One time, when we were in a market, she saw a tablecloth that she wanted. She showed it to me, and then we walked away. I went back, but wasn't sure of the size, so I went to her to clarify what size she wanted. I then went back to pick it up. What we didn't know was that we were being watched from an overhead window. After I picked it up, I had an uneasy feeling, so I went and told Mom that I was going to leave the store with the tablecloth ahead of her.

On the way out of the store, two men walked up beside me and ushered me back into the store, and then they directed me toward a back room. There they asked many questions, including if I was working alone. I told them that I was doing it alone. They asked if the woman I was with was my mother. I told them that I had done it on my own, and Mom knew nothing of what I had done. They had also picked her up and brought her into another room to ask her some questions. She assured them she knew nothing of what I had done. They warned me never to do it again, and then let me go. The store also released Mom. It was just like she had said. I was relieved, but so embarrassed that I never wanted to go back into that store. Again, as strange as it may seem, this was bonding. We stole in this manner quite often, but after this, Mom would make sure she left and was out of sight first. We were usually getting clothes she wanted. I really had little desire to steal by myself. It seemed that she was more pleased with me once we started stealing together. It also seemed that she wanted me to be obedient, but not necessarily morally good. When I went to a community church for a short time, she referred to me as a "Miss Goodie Two Shoes." That hurt a lot, but I didn't say anything.

Lots of times, I felt like Mom didn't like me for some reason. That really hurt because she always seemed to like Arlin. Later, she told me she preferred him because he was a boy. Well, that sure didn't make me feel any better. If I ever said anything about being hurt, Mom would make me feel it was as if I was just having a self-pity party. I learned to bury how I felt, and finally was able to shut down my feelings to some degree. But, sometimes I would just have a really good pity party! It never seemed to do any good though. It just made me feel worse.

I was often sick as a child. I had rheumatic fever when I was five and San Joaquin Valley Fever when I was twelve. Right after recuperating from Valley Fever, I told Mom that Dad was making advances toward me again. He must have denied it because she threatened to take me to have a lie detector test. I agreed to go, but we just drove around town like we were going, and we never went. Instead, I was sent to live with Aunt Myrte and Uncle Vernon and their three children in Sacramento. After a few months with my aunt and uncle, I went back to live with Mom and Dad. For several years, my health seemed normal, but at the end of my sophomore year I was sick again and had to have a home tutor my junior year. The doctor restricted me to bed rest because of a rheumatic heart condition. This was really hard on Mom because I was under her feet all the time.

The Last Slap

Dad continued to make advances toward me, even though I was resisting. So at sixteen, the summer before my senior year, I left home to become a housekeeper and a live-in nanny for a wonderful Jewish family of four, soon to be five. It was really nice working for them, but I had a few things to learn. I learned that you don't blow out the candle if it is left burning on a Friday night. It's mitzvah, a commandment of God, to light candles to usher in the Shabbat, or day of rest. Baby boys are often circumcised at home eight days after they are born, and some are not given their name until then. The family celebrated the circumcision of their baby boy with a big party. They also had a big bar mitzvah party for the older boy when he turned thirteen. They told me that he was then considered an adult. I learned that young Jewish girls can take Hebrew classes, and they may also have a party at twelve. At that time, they are considered old enough and responsible enough to make their own decisions. These parties were like coming of age parties. Another thing I learned was that all men didn't wear skivvies; some wore boxer shorts. Mom had taught me well how to clean house and do laundry, but I had to learn that boxer shorts are not just flimsy shorts that needed a lot of starch. And I found out that the men who wear them didn't really appreciate the starch anyway.

The job only paid nine dollars a week, but I had a place to live, wonderful food, and could finish high school. Out of the nine dollars, I managed to save enough to buy a 1937 Ford coupe for thirty-five dollars. Lots of times it didn't want to start, so I started parking it on a little hill. I would help it get rolling, then hop in and pop the clutch. It started every time. For me, it seemed that my time with this family was a time of favor. That year I won a blue ribbon in the science fair at Pacific High School. I had injected mice with cancer and fed them various diets to see if different proteins (amino acids) had an effect on the growth of the cancer. After so many weeks I removed the cancer, weighed and measured it and compared them one against the other.

That same year a friend of mine dared me to enter the Miss Colton beauty contest. I did, and much to my surprise, I won. I also experienced a peace that I had never known and saw true love within a family. It wasn't until living with this *normal* family that I realized how messed up my family life and relationships had been.

All was wonderful until about a month before graduation when I was in an auto accident. It put me in the hospital for over a month with a concussion, a severe whiplash, and a messed up back. While I was in the hospital, Mom left Dad for the last time. She wanted me to live with her to help pay the rent. So, I quit my job as housekeeper and nanny to move in with her. Shortly after I got out of the hospital, I started looking for another job. At that time, it always seemed easy to get a job; just look in the paper then go for an interview. I had mostly recovered from the accident and was physically strong so I applied at Vic Tanny's Gym. They hired me to be an instructor. Mom was also physically fit and got a job there, too, and there she met her next husband, Bill.

Mom and I had lived together for only a few months when she and Bill got married, and we moved into his home. After they married, my relationship with Mom once again seemed strained. They had only been married a couple months when Bill's three daughters, Mom, and I were all talking in the living room. I can't remember what we were talking about, but it seemed like a normal, run-of-the-mill conversation. Mom and I were standing in the middle of the room when suddenly I felt that familiar sting across my face. I was stunned. I gritted my teeth then slowly turned my head for her to slap the other cheek. I waited for a short time, but she didn't move. I silently gathered my things and walked out, never to live with her again.

Maybe it would help the reader to understand her better if I said something more about Mom. Her father played the fiddle and was a caller for dances. So when Mom was just a little girl, her mother would gather all the children and take them to the dances. Mom grew up loving to dance, and she clogged and square danced into her seventies. I also remember going to dances where my grandpa was playing the fiddle and calling for square dances. Arlin and I would dance and play and finally fall asleep on quilts under the wooden benches while Mom would continue to dance.

Joy Gartman

Mom's mother died while giving birth to a baby boy when Mom was twelve. Her older sister had already married and she, too, died a couple years later while giving birth to her first child. Her sister's baby also died. Mom and her three younger brothers were put into an orphanage for a short time because Mom's father was an alcoholic and unable to care for them. After about six months, the children were sent to various family members to be raised. Mom and the baby were sent to a "Christian" aunt and uncle. A short time later, the uncle raped Mom. The scar of that went with her to her death. It also jaded her view of Christians and men. As that young girl she decided that she couldn't trust Christians, and she had very little respect for men.

Joy — 1959

Onions to Eat

Before I left Mom and Bill's home, Mom had talked to me about a young man who worked at the gym. She really thought he was a great "catch" and that I should get to know him, so I did. Love wasn't much of a factor. Mom had said it, and for some strange reason, I was still trying to please her and earn her acceptance. Hal and I married a short time later; I was just eighteen. I had received about $5,000 from the auto accident, so we bought a car and moved to Carmel, California, an artist community, because, at heart, Hal was an artist. We lived there a few months, but the money was going quickly, so we moved to Sacramento. I was already pregnant.

Hal and I could no longer afford a phone, so the same aunt and uncle that I had lived with decided to visit us unannounced. Hal wasn't home. For some reason, Aunt Myrte decided to go into the kitchen. When she did, she opened the refrigerator; it was empty except for a few onions. Then she quickly opened the cabinets. They, too, were empty. She spun around and demanded, "What are you eating?" "Onions," I replied. "How long have you been eating just onions?" She snapped. "Just for a few days," I said, meekly. So right then, right there, they decided that I was to go with them. We left immediately. They went back later and picked up my few things. Since I was already five or six months pregnant, they were concerned about both me and the baby. Within a couple of weeks, my aunt and uncle had found a place for me to live and have the baby in Southern California. So, I was loaded on a bus and sent to a home for unwed mothers. Most of the residents were unmarried, pregnant girls about my age. Interestingly enough, I was the social outcast because I was the only one who was married and planning on keeping the baby.

It wasn't long before Hal was there, knocking at the door and wanting to see me. My aunt and uncle had told him that he had to have a dependable job before I would go back with him, so he joined the Air Force. He had been in the service before and had served in the Korean War. He was now assigned to a base at Biloxi, Mississippi, so off we went all the way across the country. By now, I was eight months pregnant and huge. It was a long trip, but all went well. My beautiful little girl, Tracy, was born a month later. Shortly after her birth, I started having seizures. I was diagnosed with epilepsy. The doctor said that the seizures were possibly caused from the auto accident. I was nineteen when Tracy was born.

Hal was in training for less than a year when he was assigned to Opheim, Montana. For some reason, I can't remember now— maybe the availability of housing— Tracy and I stayed in California for a short time before we drove up to a tiny town 50 miles north of Glasgow and just eight miles south of the Canadian border. That winter, it got down to 40 below zero, and that's cold! At first, we lived on the military site outside of town in a

28-foot trailer. Hal worked at the site, but I soon got a job at the bowling alley in town. The bowling alley also had a grill and diner. I worked wherever I was needed. They were usually very busy because they were the only entertainment in town. Before long, we moved into town across the street from my work. We lived in an upstairs one-bedroom apartment with a shared bathroom down the hall.

Although Hal was now providing for the family, he was still struggling in other areas. At times he would wake up screaming, and he would have frequent outbursts of rage; his unpredictable behavior was unnerving for me. In short, I was afraid of Hal. Once he choked me until I lost consciousness. While I was passed out, I saw myself in a little boat all alone in a vast ocean. When I regained consciousness, it seemed that he hadn't known what he was doing. A couple other times when I returned home, there were marks on Tracy. He said that she had just fallen. I wasn't sure. His mother said that he was different after the Korean War and after the "mysterious" death of his son. Her statement always concerned me, but I never asked the questions that were running through my mind. One night, he told me that he was going to kill me. He also told me that he had thought about it and had reasoned that if they killed him, he would be with his son. And if they put him in prison, he would have his art. I was terrified!

I had no idea what triggered his behavior. I just knew I wanted to get Tracy and me as far from there as I could. But how and when could we go? The only person I knew to call was Dad. He agreed to come right away. We left the day after he came while Hal was still at work. We left and I never looked back, and I never regretted leaving. I had been living in terror for months, even afraid to go to work and leave Tracy with him. When we got to California, I was still afraid that he would come after us. Several years later, Tracy found out that shortly after we left, he was discharged from the military on a mental medical, and he did return to California just a few miles away from where we were living.

From Frying Pan to Fire

My brother had remained friends with Dale, a guy I had dated before I met Hal. One day, the two of them came over to visit. Dale was in the Navy and was going to Hawaii, and he wanted to marry me. My half-brother, Roy (Dad's middle child from a previous marriage) warned me that I was jumping from the frying pan into the fire. However, Hawaii seemed a long way away from Hal and a safe place to be, so I got a six-week divorce in Las Vegas. Tracy and I were on our way to Hawaii. I was twenty-one. Shaun was born August of the following year, and David was born November of the next year.

Dale was on submarines and was out to sea several months at a time. Soon I got a job teaching school. I had accumulated a couple years of college. So, like I had always done, I read the ad in the paper and went in for an interview. I got the teaching job with the condition that I would take at least two college courses each year. I agreed to do so, and they gave me a provisional teaching credential. I went to work. I loved teaching school. I taught while I was pregnant, even into the eighth month with Shaun and through most of my pregnancy with David. Muumuus were great for hiding the cargo.

While in Hawaii, I still had the seizures, but added to them were severe migraine headaches. Even though Tracy was very young, she was always mommy's little helper, especially when I had headaches. Tracy also started kindergarten in Hawaii. What I didn't know at the time was that Dale was molesting her. I was very suspicious and had at one time even asked Tracy, but at the time I asked her, she denied that anything had happened. What I found out later was that she had been threatened and was afraid to tell me. What a generational curse! First Mom, then me, now Tracy, and then later one of my granddaughters would be date raped. In four generations, three of us had been raped, and all of us had been sexually abused.

While in Hawaii, I had made friends with several of the "submarine widows," as we were sometimes called because of being alone so much. We started doing lots of things together when the guys were gone out to sea, like going shopping with all of the kids, going out to eat with the all of the kids, or taking all of the kids to the beach.

One time, a couple of these friends asked if I wanted to go out dancing and have some fun. I loved to dance. At the time, it seemed like a good idea so I agreed to go. Little did I imagine that this would lead to an affair, and not only an affair, but another pregnancy and a baby boy. Much to my regret and shame, I had repeated the sin of my mother! Shortly, after I discovered that I was pregnant, we—Tracy, Shaun, David, and pregnant me—flew back to California. I was gone again and I didn't look back. Dru was born in San Bernardino a few months later. I was twenty-five, was on my own with four children, and had already had two failed marriages. What a mess I was making of my life!

White Trash

After Dru was born, I quickly landed a job at juvenile hall and hired a live-in babysitter. Even though I had a good job, it didn't seem like there was enough money to make ends meet. One afternoon, I was complaining to God that He didn't pay my bills, so I was considering becoming a prostitute. At one time, Mom had mentioned that I could make good money at prostituting in someplace like Las Vegas. Of course, my dad would have been delighted. As I was musing on these thoughts, my neighbor knocked on my back door. I opened the door to see her hand extended to me with a check for fifteen dollars. She and her husband felt like they wanted to give me their tithe. I was speechless and in tears. How did they know that at that exact time those thoughts were going through my mind? I was so touched that they would care, and even more amazed at God's loving intervention. This was an incident that I would not forget. My neighbor never brought another check, and I didn't become a prostitute. Thank God.

A Heathen with God

Like my heathen parents, I, too, was a heathen. There had been a few brushes with God. In high school, I had written a paper for my English class on "If I only had an hour to live." I remember that the main part of the paper was lamenting because I couldn't believe in Jesus. And then there were my aunt and uncle who lived in Sacramento, the ones that I was sent to live with when I was eleven. They were Christians. I remember enjoying going to their church. It was a small church. I really liked the music and my Sunday school teacher, Doris.

I also enjoyed going to Colton Community Church for a short time when I was in high school. They had a great youth group. The summer before my sophomore year, they were all going up into the mountains to a campground called Forest Home, and I really wanted to go. Mom and Dad didn't have money to send me, so I went up and down the streets in a nice neighborhood asking if I could work in order to earn enough money to pay the registration fees. One lady hired me to do some sweeping and to clean her windows inside and out and wash her screens. I was delighted and worked really hard, but didn't make enough for the trip. I was disappointed. But when I went to church the following Sunday, I found out that she had gone to the church and paid the rest of my fees. WOW! I went and had a great time. At one campfire meeting, they had a speaker followed by an altar call. The speaker wanted us to commit our lives to Jesus. I was touched but remember this flash of a thought "I want to have fun." I didn't raise my hand. I can't say that I believed in Jesus, but I really did feel the presence of the Holy Spirit. For the next ten years, no one witnessed to me—not even the Jehovah Witnesses or Mormons—not even the Mormons. I was left alone to have my "fun." I had believed the lie of the world about what constitutes fun. God had given me free will and I had chosen to do it my way. I cannot tell you how many times I have looked back on that choice to have "fun" with regret.

Another one of my brushes with God was when I was dating a Catholic. I had gone to a Catholic church a few times and had started going through a catechism class. But when I went to the church once to talk to one of the priests, he and another priest were drunk. I was disappointed and quit the class. Nothing had really connected. For some reason, I always believed in God as Father and Creator—don't know why—but I couldn't believe in Jesus as "His only begotten Son." On my first Christmas after moving back to California, about the same time as the neighbor's tithe incident, someone sent me a special Christmas card about *The Carpenter*. I posted that card by my phone and would read it every so often. But I still couldn't believe, and my life didn't change. Since I was unable to figure it out in my mind, it was impossible to for me to believe—it just didn't make any sense to me. It was impossible for me to get beyond my reasoning. I continued to work, to raise my children, and had begun to date.

Cinderella

There were a couple of guys at work, one a psychologist and the other a counselor. I went out with each of them a couple of times, but nothing serious. I also dated someone who raced cross-country motorcycles, and I had started going with him to races in the desert. There I met Carl, a hard-headed, loud, but loveable German. He was good-looking and fun to be with. At first I was just fascinated, but then I began to get serious. Carl had never been married and wasn't looking to be married. On the other hand, I had not only been married before, but also had four young ones. I don't know how long we dated before I began to think of a deeper commitment. Marriage wasn't on his radar. I had always been somewhat pragmatic, and now I needed to consider the kids. Even though my heart wanted to continue to be with Carl, I decided that I couldn't just go on dating. I needed to settle down. So I went to him and told him, and if I remember correctly, I didn't hear from him for a while.

The only times that I remembered praying before was when I was pregnant with the children. I prayed that they would be healthy. I didn't pray to Jesus, I only prayed to God the Father, and my children were all healthy! This time I also prayed to God the Father. Not that I really knew how to pray, but I told Him that

I would go back to Dale if He wanted me to, but God would have to make me willing. I also told Him that if He wanted me to marry one of the other guys that I had dated, I would; but who I really wanted to marry was Carl. Maybe because I didn't pray often, it felt as though God and heaven had all stopped to listen. God answered my prayer! I knew that He heard, and I knew that He cared. It seemed like a long time, but it was only a couple of weeks later when Carl came over with an engagement ring and asked me to marry him. I couldn't have been happier. God answered my prayer, even though we were both heathens.

At that time, the kids and I lived in Rialto and Carl lived and worked fifty miles away near Los Angeles. Soon, we were buying a house, planning a wedding, and moving. We bought a house on a hill in La Crescenta that overlooked the Los Angeles basin. All was like a dream come true. I felt a lot like how Cinderella may have felt. I didn't need to work anymore and could be a wife and a stay-at-home mom. Our live-in babysitter even moved with us. I was so very happy.

When Carl and I got married, it was as if my whole life had changed. I was nobody; he was somebody—successful and important. He was the owner of a die-casting company. I had always been poor; he was well off. It was easy for me to become Mrs. Him. Whatever he wanted to do, I wanted to do; wherever he wanted to go, I wanted to go. I loved it. I didn't mind forgetting who I was. I had taken on his identity.

Carl liked hunting and fishing, and I did, too. He included me and usually the kids in his activities. We went to Europe and vacationed in Mexico a lot, sometimes just the two of us, but usually as a family. We went to parties, and we had parties. It was a "fun" time. I also got heavily involved in the occult, such as astrology, card and palm readings, the readings of Edgar Cayce and others, and I was going to fortune-tellers. I even had a party were we had four fortune-tellers at the house to tell the future of those who attended. A couple of people were upset. One guy even pushed one of the fortune tellers into the pool. I'm not sure what happened. There was always plenty to drink, so we blamed it on the booze. Ron and Edith McManus, who lived up the street from us, were also at the party.

Snow White

Ron and Edith had five children, as I remember; one was a daughter the same age as Tracy and they fast became friends. They went to church as a family, and they asked us if they could take all four of the kids to church with them. They usually went out to lunch afterwards. It was great! Carl and I enjoyed our leisurely Sunday mornings together. This went on for some time. Then Tracy went to camp one summer and got "saved" and baptized. It seemed to me that after that she started getting pushy, wanting to pray at meals, even in public. I remember being so embarrassed, and it seemed like she prayed forever. She also started pushing me to go to church with her; she even wanted me and the boys to get baptized.

I really liked Edith and even her faith. She was a nice person. Her parents were from the Netherlands and had gone to Argentina as missionaries. On one occasion, she asked me about my faith. I told her that I admired her, but I didn't know how she could believe that stuff about Jesus being the only Son of God. I was completely serious. She was just as serious when she told me that she didn't know how I couldn't believe. I was stunned. She really believed. It caused me to think, think a lot, and for quite some time.

I finally agreed to get baptized and to allow the boys to be baptized, even though I still didn't believe. Edith went to a Pentecostal church and that was where they were taking the kids. So we signed up to be baptized. At the baptism, the pastor was asking those being baptized about their faith in Jesus. I didn't understand the question, so I just stated my name. He stalled a little, but then went ahead and baptized me. As I came up out of the water, I was speaking in a language I didn't understand and…. I was saying "Jesus, Jesus, Jesus." What amazed me most was that I was saying Jesus because I still didn't believe that He was the only Son of God. Questions were firing in my mind about this experience and about what was coming out of my mouth: Why was I saying Jesus? What was this that sounded like another language?

A short time later, I had another "talk" with Creator, Father God; I still didn't know how to pray. I told him that if Jesus really was His only Son and if He really was my only way to be saved, I really wanted to know. Nothing seemed to happen until about six months later. One day when I opened a Bible someone had given me, a heavenly being appeared right beside me. The scripture I had opened to was about the woman at the well with Jesus. She had come to fetch water and met Jesus sitting on the edge of the well. Jesus "read her mail." He told her how many times she had been married and that she was shacking up with another man right then. This got her attention and mine too! I had also been previously married and had had an affair. Then she asked Him a question about where to serve God. He didn't say where, but he told her how. She was to worship him in Spirit and in Truth.

At that point, I knew that people were to worship Jesus with their spirits—not with their minds. That was a relief to me because I had been trying to make sense of the Christian experience. "Jesus is the TRUTH." I didn't hear an outward voice, but the inward voice was loud and clear. A lot of other things were imparted to my mind, like how much Jesus loved me, like I didn't have to figure it out, I could just believe. And I did believe. Before that encounter, I could not believe; after that encounter, I could not help but to believe. I knew! I just knew! I knew that it was true and that Jesus was Truth.

I can't explain how it happened, but I was a new person. Sorrow filled my heart for my sins, for my rebellion, for my involvement with the occult, for sexual sins, for having had an affair, for not believing or accepting Jesus, and for not accepting the love that God so freely offered. I wept and told the Father *and Jesus* how sorry I was for what I all the bad things that I had ever done. And if they would help me I wouldn't do them anymore. My life had been a lifetime of sin. I knew right then that—because of the price Jesus paid—I was fully forgiven. Forgiven of everything! I had encountered the grace of God. It was as if I had been washed as white as snow. I no longer felt dirty. Something glorious had happened!!!

The Risk of Loving

At first, Carl didn't say much, but as time went on, my being a Christian seemed to get under his skin. Then, one Christmas day while he was talking to Mom, he said, "Your daughter has gotten religion." Mom wasn't keen on Christianity either, but she didn't want to make waves, so she replied, "Oh, she'll get over it." From their conversation, one might have thought that instead of becoming a Christian, I had the three-day measles and would get over it in a short time. Their whole dialogue seemed odd, because I was right there with them, but they were talking around me like I was a sack of potatoes. I said nothing, and they soon dropped the subject.

Later, Carl began putting limitations on me. The first thing to be limited was my giving to the church. He informed me that I could give no more than a dollar a week. By that time, I had learned that wives were to submit to their husbands, so I didn't argue. I wasn't happy, but I obeyed and gave only a dollar a week. One Sunday morning, as the offering basket was being passed, Patty, a friend of mine, leaned over and whispered in my ear that the Lord had told her to tell me that *obedience was better than sacrifice*. At the time, Patty knew nothing of what Carl had told me. I knew I was doing the right thing. Sometimes he wanted to go to a party or a movie that was off-color; I would go, but I would silently pray. The Lord impressed upon me heavily that I was to submit, and without argument, so I did. The Lord gave such grace and such love at that time.

Love had been an issue in my life. I didn't know that I couldn't fully love. As an adult, I realized that, something had happened when I was three years old. Mom had left Dad and remarried a man named Ray. I didn't consciously remember him, but shortly after I became a Christian, I had a recollection of a scene when I was little. A man was standing in a living room holding me. I was crying because he was leaving Mom, Arlin, and me. As that little girl, I loved him and had accepted him as my daddy, and the thought of him leaving was extremely painful. Then I knew that the little girl in me had made a decision to never love anyone again because it hurt too much to lose them. To my knowledge, Mom had never mentioned that incident, but this vision was so clear. When I asked her about it, she told me that it was true and told me that his name was Ray. She explained that she had loved him, but she wanted him to leave because she didn't like how he treated Arlin. She also confirmed that I was three years old at the time he left.

Remembering that event was very significant because I realized that I had never felt like I had truly been "in love." I also found it extremely difficult to receive love. Even with Carl, I was happy, and I really cared, and deep inside I knew that I loved him, but there always seemed to be a lid on my love emotions. The Lord led me into asking Him to forgive me, not as an adult, but as the wounded little Joy inside me. She asked Jesus to forgive her for not wanting to ever love again. Then she asked Him to let her love. The little girl had been afraid and didn't want to risk the pain of loving, but at the same time she felt so much of the love of the Heavenly Father that she felt safe.

It was as if pure waves of His love swept over me. I was assured of God's love for me and knew that even if loving did end up hurting again, I must take the risk and choose love. How could I not when I had received His great love? The blockage had been removed. Love gushed up and out of me. I loved the children as I had never loved them before. Love was like a river coming out of me for Carl, people, life, and Jesus. Love filled my heart to overflowing. It was real, it was deep, and it was indescribable.

Signs and Wonders

Not only was there this awesome love coming out of me, there was also a deep hunger within me. I had been spiritually malnourished for over thirty years, and I craved lots of spiritual food. I had an insatiable appetite for the Bible, and for Christian books and tapes, which I would read and listen to in the mornings while the kids were in school. Except for church on Sunday morning, my Christian activities were limited to the weekdays while Carl was at work. I went to a Wednesday morning Bible study with two Pentecostal ladies, attended the Pasadena daytime Women's Aglow, and visited and prayed with my Christian friends.

One time when I was at the Pentecostal Bible study, we were praying for a nun who had cancer in her right lung. All of a sudden, I had this flash of a picture of Jesus' hand reaching into her lung and pulling out the cancer. This may have been the first time anything like this happened to me, because I was too afraid to share.

The two ladies began to teach their forty-five minute lesson about if God gives you a gift or shows you something, then you need to share that with the body. Finally, when they finished, I timidly raised my hand and shared what I had seen. That was a few weeks before Christmas. We took a six-week break for the holidays. When we returned six weeks later, the nun was there at our meeting to tell us what had happened. When she went back to have further tests, they found that all the cancer was completely gone from her lung. I was amazed, amazed at what had happened and amazed at the love and the power of God. God also healed me of the migraine headaches and the epilepsy that had plagued me since Tracy was born.

At this same Pentecostal meeting, they were going to pray for someone's leg to grow out because it was a couple inches shorter than her other leg. Silently, I thought to myself, "This I've got to see," so I positioned myself on the floor right by her legs. I didn't really believe that it would grow. When they started praying, nothing happened. A thought darted through my mind, "See, it didn't grow." But right then, one of the ladies stopped everything and said that someone there didn't believe. Conviction pierced me and I immediately repented. While my eyes were open and I was silently repenting, the leg shot out. It grew! In a flash, doubt was changed to faith!

After about six months of being a Christian, the priest at Saint Luke's Episcopal Church asked me to co-teach a daytime Bible Study with my friend and prayer partner, Patty. Patty was a cradle Episcopalian. We both had recently been Spirit-filled, we were both prophetic, and we both believed that we could do anything the Bible said we could do in Jesus Name.

At that time, God showed me that spirits of lust and rejection had entered me at the time of my conception. Patty and I agreed to fast and pray, because we had heard that some demons won't come out unless you do; that when you fast and pray, this is more authority in the name of Jesus to cast out the unclean spirits. Patty and I prayed and took authority, and I was delivered of spirits of lust and rejection that had been with me throughout my life. I was being liberated. Patty and I would also pray often in the Holy Spirit before we were to teach the class, and the Lord would give us what we needed to teach.

After I became a Christian, I began to see things about an individual when I was praying for them. Then I would pray out loud what I saw. The people would often cry because it would be exactly what they were thinking or needing. Since I had not been raised in a church and didn't have any Christian experience with which to compare, this all seemed to be normal Christianity. I thought that all Christians could see as I was seeing and hear what I was hearing. I also thought that they were all having visions and dreams. Therefore, when we were teaching in the Episcopal Church, there was this assumption, on my part, that everyone moved in these gifts of the Spirit. No one in the class ever said anything. They just listened intently. We talked about things that were prophetic, and we shared the dreams or the visions that we were having. Only God knows what they were thinking. But they kept coming, and the class seemed to be growing. Sometimes I think that God chuckles at our naïveté—and He uses it.

One time, it seemed like the Lord wanted me to take an apple to the class. I balked at first, but then prayed to God that if Cherie, another Spirit-filled Episcopalian, offered me an apple, I would take it to the Bible study. Sure enough, her daughter pulled a tiny little apple out of a bag to show me. I commented to her daughter about it being cute, and then for some unknown reason Cherie offered me an apple. So I took that apple to class and had others also share. They shared about how the seeds within an apple produce seeds for other apple trees, and about how the Christ-seed that resides inside Christians produces a Christ-likeness within their lives. We also shared about how the Christ-seeds that are in us are to be shared with others so that those seeds can bring forth the gospel of salvation to the lost. God was teaching us as we were teaching others.

We believed for signs and wonders, and God didn't disappoint us because they were happening quite often. One day, I was visiting Patty when her husband, Pete, was home. We were all standing in the living room when they started talking about a tree in their front yard. They wanted it removed. One of us remembered that Jesus had said if someone really believed, they could speak to a mulberry tree, and it could be cast into the sea. We really believed, so the three of us looked at the tree, and told it "Be removed, in the Name of Jesus." Nothing seemed to happen… until the next morning. It was struck to the ground by lightening. It was removed! We weren't surprised because we had believed. We just rejoiced at how God had answered our prayer.

The Pasadena Women's Aglow asked me to teach a Catholic women's Bible study connected with their organizations. One day we got on the subject of baptism, and many of the women attending had been baptized as infants, but they all wanted to be re-baptized as adults. I told them that I would baptize them only if they got permission from their priest. There were twelve of them who agreed to talk to their priest, but we decided that first we would all fast and pray. Much to their surprise, the priest said that it would be okay. He said that he would give them permission because the Church was going to celebrate the baptism of John the Baptist the following Sunday. But we knew that the reason he had given them permission was because God had answered our prayers. I had never baptized anyone in my life, and the only baptism I could remember seeing was my own. One of the ladies suggested that we use her pool, so we did. On a beautiful sunny day I had the honor of baptizing twelve on-fire Catholic ladies. The eldest was in her eighties.

In Love but Rejected

All of this spiritual stuff was going on during the weekdays but life at home remained much the same. Carl and I still went to Mexico, we still went hunting and fishing, and still had lots of fun. But I had changed, and he didn't like the change. When he was grumbling one time, I told him that I was a much better wife after I had become a Christian, because I was more agreeable. He wasn't impressed. I was different and he knew it. After a couple of years, more edicts were given. Anything to do with Christianity had to fit into ten hours a week. He reasoned that Catholics did it in an hour a week, so ten hours a week should be plenty of time for me to complete my Christian duties. This meant not only meetings, but reading, praying, and any phone calls or visits that had anything to do with my faith or Christian friends. My closest friends were all Christians. It was getting harder, but I complied and I prayed. Then he forbade me and the kids to go to church on Sundays. I prayed more, and I complained to God especially about the kids not going to church, but I felt strongly that I needed to obey. I needed to submit, and submit I did, but only by God's grace.

Then, at the dinner table on Thanksgiving Day of 1977, after more than seven years of marriage, Carl blurted out, "Either change your religion or change your residence!" He was serious. I was stunned; the kids were silent. After dinner, he went upstairs to watch TV. My mind was racing as Tracy and I cleaned the kitchen. I didn't want to leave! Nor could I deny my faith! I quietly joined him, and begged him not to give me an ultimatum —because I would have to choose God. He wouldn't budge. I cried until my eyes were almost swollen shut. I had believed that he would be saved, especially since God had allowed me to marry him. Nonetheless, before Christmas, the four kids and I were moved out of the house. I was in a daze. My Cinderella life had come to an end. Even though Carl has come near death, he remains unsaved to this day.

The children and I spent Christmas in a rented house at the bottom of the hill. Life changed—no longer a house on the top of the hill, no more live-in babysitter. No more Carl. No more private schools for the boys. During the following summer break, we moved up to Sacramento. This also meant no more cheerleading and being mascot of the high school for Tracy. The kids were uprooted again. I had dragged my children from one failed relationship to another. They were suffering from my choices. Each of them was getting wounded and scarred, and it seemed that there was very little I could do.

When we first moved to Sacramento, we lived next door to my Aunt Myrte; Uncle Vernon had died of cancer several years earlier. After a short time we found Trinity Church, and it became our church home. I got a job selling manufactured homes, and the kids and I moved into another rented house. Furthermore, the

White Trash

kids talked me into getting a little shaggy dog from the pound named Wiggles.

Dru, David Shannon, Joy, Shaun, Tracy, 1979

I Had a Dream

An 1979, Tracy graduated from high school. That fall Tracy and I both enrolled full-time at Trinity Bible College. I had already taken a class in the fall of 1978 and one in the spring of 1979. I continued to work. There at Trinity, Tracy met Tony, her future husband. Tony was from Hawaii, so after graduation, he and Tracy went there to marry, to have their honeymoon, and to live. Their oldest daughter, Bethany, was also born there.

Steve, a tall, handsome man, was also attending Trinity Bible College at that time; however, marriage wasn't on my radar, and I didn't pay much attention to anyone. Almost everyone was younger, and besides, for me there was school, there was work, and there was raising my four children. I had a few friends; outside of that, there was little time in my life for anything else. But one night I had a dream. In the dream, I was sitting on the back row of a church when I found out that a wedding was taking place. I casually wondered about who was getting married. A father figure, not my earthly father, came up to me and wanted to walk me to the front of the church. In the dream, I knew that it was my heavenly Father, even though he looked just like an earthly man. Then I realized that it was my wedding. I was puzzled and most interested because I wasn't dating anyone at the time. I was straining to see who the groom was, but couldn't see his face. Then my heavenly Father and I turned a corner as we got to the front, and Steve was standing there. I just hid the dream in my heart. But I did move to the other side of the class, just a couple rows behind Steve so that I could check him out. At the Christmas break, Steve left school and moved back to Nevada. I had no way of contacting him, but it was okay. God had given me perfect peace either way, whether he stayed in Nevada or returned to class. When school resumed, Steve still had not returned. Then two weeks after the classes began, there he was sitting in his usual place as if it were the first day back to school. We had been friends and had talked often about school and the like, but after his return from Nevada we started dating and spending lots more time with each other.

Steve and I were married in June of 1980 and were ordained into the Evangelical Church Alliance in 1981. The Assemblies of God would not ordain me or Steve because I had been previously married, even though Steve had never been married before. I felt guilt and shame and real sorrow for him; he was such a good man. Now not only was Steve married to someone who had been previously divorced, he had also inherited four teenagers. Marrying into a ready-made family with four teenagers would prove to be the greatest challenge of his life.

In many ways, Steve was the opposite of Carl. Carl was blue-eyed and blonde. Steve had large brown eyes and almost black hair. Steve was an introvert, quiet and reserved, whereas Carl was outgoing, bold, and at times, a bit noisy. Most importantly, however, Steve was not only a Christian, he was called to ministry. For me this was very important because I also felt a call of God on my life.

In other ways, Steve and Carl were similar. They both loved the out-of-doors; they liked fishing, hunting, and motorcycles. Both were exceptionally firm with the boys; at times I felt they were overly strict.

Run for Your Life

Steve loved Nevada, and had lived there before Bible college. He wanted to return. He found a job at a mine in Gabbs, Nevada. Tracy had already moved to Hawaii, so three teenage boys, Wiggles, Steve and I moved into a 10 by 60 foot trailer; that is only 600 square feet for five grown people and a dog. The trailer was over-crowded and depressing, and we didn't even have a yard. Right behind our trailer was an old filthy dog kennel about eight feet wide by twelve feet long. At one time it probably had been used for a storage shed. Shaun decided to fix it up for a place for him to stay. He put cardboard over the dirt floor, and then he went to our storage shed and found lots of treasures including pieces of carpet to cover the cardboard and an electric cord as a plug for a lamp and clock-radio. He also discovered a bed and a night stand and even pictures for the wall. He did an excellent job, especially considering what he had to work with. Many days, after the kids left for school and Steve had gone to work, I would cry.

I wasn't the only one having a difficult time adjusting. At sixteen, Shaun ran away from home to go back to California. He later joined the circus and traveled throughout the U.S. and Canada. He also lived on the streets of San Francisco. I prayed. Before

Shaun left home, I had a dream of him going down into a manhole. In the dream, I was able to follow him just enough to see what it was like down there. There was a whole underworld, dark and foreboding, but the Lord told me not to pray him out of his choices. Shaun made some very unwise decisions, but he was in the Lord's hands.

Steve was an honorable man and wanted to adopt the children. He adopted David and Dru while we were still in Gabbs. Shaun had already run away from home, so he wasn't adopted until later. Tracy was already married and elected not to be adopted. Bless Steve's heart! Not only did he want to become a true father to the children, he was also trying to cover the shame of all my marriages and my messed up life.

David also left home at sixteen to train as a diesel mechanic. After he finished his training, he moved back to Sacramento where he was hired to work on equipment for a carnival. I prayed more. An interesting observation: I had left home at sixteen and now two of the boys had also left home at sixteen. It is very difficult for a mother to let go, but God gave me the grace. When David left home, I was more concerned for him because he never seemed as savvy or as confident as Shaun. I was worried about his ability to survive on his own, especially at such a young age. I needed several extra helpings of God's grace, and God was always faithful to give them.

At times, I wouldn't hear from either of the boys for months. When I worried, I recommitted them into the hands of my Lord. Sometimes I would pray that one or the other of them would just phone so I could be assured that they were alright—and they would call. One night I had a dream about David getting AIDS. I wasn't so worried about David and homosexuality, but I was worried about him using drugs. It was almost more than I could handle. I prayed, "Lord, just let him call so I can tell him the dream." He called, and I told him. His silence was telling.

Later he told me that a couple of homosexuals had picked him up off the streets of Santa Cruz, and he was staying at their house. He also said that when I told him my dream, he was terrified. He picked up the few things that he had and ran. He ran until he could run no more. He would stumble, then he would get up again and run some more. Finally, completely exhausted and out of wind, he staggered onto a lawn. He leaned up against their sign to catch his breath. When he recovered a bit, he looked at the sign. It was a sign in front of a church.

An elderly couple from the church ended up inviting David to live in their home. They were very nurturing, and they helped him get his life back together. After a few months, they drove him to our house in Sacramento. He was a changed young man. Shaun and David both had their share of digging in garbage cans and shivering during cold nights outdoors. Thank God for His mercy and His grace, not only for them, but for me too. During that time, I learned to trust in God, and I learned the incredible value of praying, "Not my will, but the will of the Father." I knew in my heart that God loved them more than I loved them. He loved them with an eternal love, a strong love, a love that would allow them to fall, but it was also a love that would always hear them if they called. I also knew that if I prayed in my own understanding, it could be to their eternal detriment.

How I see the faithfulness of God the Father. He was a loving Father to both Shaun and David, and they are both such godly men today!

Why These Parents?

Shortly after I became a Christian, I asked God why He had given me my parents. I was silently thinking, "God, why didn't you give me somebody like Billy Graham, or at least, you could have given me Christian parents." Immediately I had an inward voice speak to me clearly. "I didn't give you your parents for you. I gave you to your parents *for them*." The Lord even told me that I was His gift to them. At the end of 1982, this statement began to make sense.

Dad was born in February, 1903; he was sixteen years older than my mom. Now his health was failing. I was an on-fire Christian and was concerned about his eternal destination. Even after years of prayer, my dad remained a non-believer.

Mom married Tex after she divorced Bill. She and Dad probably hadn't been together for over thirty-five years when she decided to go down to Rialto and take care of him. This was while Steve, the boys and I were still living in Gabbs. I decided to drive down to visit them both. I couldn't freely talk to Dad about the condition of his soul and his need for salvation with Mom present, so I quietly prayed to have some time with him alone. A short time later Mom announced that she needed to go out for something. We were alone.

Dad knew that he was dying, so we talked a little bit about that. Then God gave me the boldness to ask him where he thought he was going to spend eternity. He was visibly shaken. I explained to him that he still had a choice in the matter. He could choose to repent of all he had ever done, and he could ask Jesus to become his Lord and Savior. He started crying, so I asked him if he wanted me to pray with him. He did; I prayed, but when we came to the part about his need of repentance, he started praying aloud by himself. With tears running down his cheeks, he started asking God to forgive him of many, many things including what he had done to me, Tracy, and others. I cried as Dad asked Jesus into his heart. He died a few weeks later, and was laid to rest on his eightieth birthday.

On the Move

While we were still in Gabbs, some people living in Empire and Gerlach, Nevada, wanted Steve and me to help them start a Protestant church. They had a Mormon and a Catholic church, but the closest protestant church was over an hour away in Reno. We had ministered at that church in Empire for a couple of years before we decided to move to Sacramento. Since we were going to move, we wanted someone to take over the church. After some time of looking and trying different possibilities, the Baptist church out of Fallon, Nevada agreed to take it on.

However, the new Baptist minister was killed in a car accident on his second trip to Empire. We later heard that he was swerving to miss an animal. Steve and I had made countless trips driving back home to Gabbs in the dark. With the dim lights on our 1966 Volkswagen, it was very hard to see at night. Sometimes we would have to swerve to miss cows sleeping on the warm road. We usually prayed before we left home, and would thank God for a safe trip when we returned. How sorry we were to hear the tragic news! But the Southern Baptists didn't give up. They soon got someone else to serve in his place. That church is still active to this day.

In the summer of Dru's junior year, we moved back to Sacramento to take a position at Orangevale Assembly of God Church. It was at the same church where Steve and I had interned while we were attending Trinity Bible College. This time there was just the three of us—Steve, Dru, and me. Dru had always been such a good kid, but he had been hidden under the strong personalities of Tracy, Shaun and David. This was the first time that he was center stage, and it was a nice time for him and for me. He got a job at Mc Donald's, and the two of us would often go out for lunch. He was a half year ahead in school when he graduated the following January. He joined the army when he was eighteen. The nest had so quickly emptied after Steve and I married. I really missed the kids.

Steve had been asked to be the principal of the elementary school in Orangevale, and they wanted me to teach math and be his administrative assistant. We also served as singles ministers and youth ministers while we were in the Sacramento area. After a couple of years Steve decided to go to work for a prison ministry called Match-2 Ministries, and was assigned to Folsom prison. I founded World Outreach in 1984. Its original intent was to call world leaders, both political and Christian, to prayer and repentance. Such a call was based on 2 Chronicles 7:14. *If my people, which are called by my name, shall humble themselves, and pray, and seek my face, and turn from their wicked ways; then will I hear from heaven, and will forgive their sin, and will heal their land.*

Thanks to Bobby and Ivan Pendell and others, World Outreach has grown considerably. We now have missionaries throughout the world, and we have orphanages in China and Kenya. Our lives were very full.

Wilderness Flowers

We had only lived in Sacramento for a few years, before Steve wanted to return to Nevada, so he started looking for a job in that direction. He found two openings for a counselor—one in Carson City and one 350 miles east in Wells. He wanted to live in rural Nevada, so in 1987 we moved to Wells, and he took a job at the Wells Conservation Camp. Wells was a town of about 1,100 people, sixty-six miles from both the Idaho and Utah borders. Wells had three casinos, two brothels, two bars, three gas stations, several motels, a forestry station, schools, and a country grocery store. The town was mainly supported by the people passing through on US 80 and Highway 93. For Steve, we were right next to heaven, lots of areas for hunting and fishing. For me, it was a wilderness. Wells was isolated, and I was far removed from my familiar Christian soundings. But it would be from this place that God would launch and direct our future lives and ministries. Seeing these new ministries develop were as if my Heavenly Father had planted flowers in my wilderness.

Our first ministry was at a house church in Frank and Marsha's home. They were both new Christians and were excited about the Holy Spirit. We became friends right away. They had started the little group with lots of zeal, but they had little experience. They asked Steve and me to take it over just a few months after we arrived. They wanted me to lead. Even though Steve would sometimes refer to himself as Pentecostal, he usually steered away from the Spirit-filled side of Christianity. Steve was drawn to the Episcopal and the Presbyterian churches; He felt more at home there. I, on the other hand, was drawn more to the evangelical and Pentecostal churches, so we both went to the Episcopal and Presbyterian churches and once in a while I would go the Assemblies of God church.

A year or so after we moved to Wells, another of the flowers of ministry developed—the Piute and Shoshone nations of Northern Nevada. I spoke in their churches, ministered at some of their regional gatherings, and did some of their funerals. One of the funerals was for an elderly princess. The place was packed. She had a full open casket and was dressed in her native clothes. She wore high-top buckskin moccasins and a red buckskin dress with lots of fringes. Her hair was long and braided, and she had on lots of turquoise. She looked beautiful.

She had just accepted the Lord two weeks before her death, so I talked about that, and talked about what advice she would want to give them now. She was in heaven, and she would want them there too. At the end, I asked them to bow their heads and close their eyes while we prayed. I asked anyone who wanted to accept Jesus as Savior and Lord to just quietly look up at me. When I looked up, there were two to three hundred dark brown eyes looking right at me. My eyes flooded with tears. It was difficult to continue because of emotion. I thought that they might have misunderstood, so I repeated the invitation to accept Jesus as Savior and Lord. When I looked up again there were even more eyes looking straight at me. What a victory in death!

When I arrived at the cemetery, the young men of her tribe had recently dug her grave. The casket was still open and many quietly placed their tokens of flowers, jewelry, pictures and the like into it. When all were through with their gifts and goodbyes the casket was closed. There were three long ropes resting under it, the ends of the ropes were neatly looped, three on each side. Six young braves stepped forward, three on each side. In unison, they picked up the ropes, and in silence with perfect unity and rhythm, they lowered her into the grave. The casket gently swung back and forth as it went down. A few family members took hands full of dirt and threw it on the casket, and then the young men came back and shoveled in the rest of the dirt. It was solemn. It was beautiful.

I have done many funerals over the years, but this one stands out in many ways. Everyone seemed like children. They so respected this princess leader; they respected God, the church and me. The customs of these dear people exhibited such grace and dignity. But most importantly, they were so receptive to accepting Jesus as Lord. They demonstrated a freedom that I had never seen. They weren't afraid of what others thought—just like little children.

By the late eighties, Steve was given a promotion that required us to move south to Ely. While there Steve went to the Episcopal Church and I attended the Assembly of God Church. I ministered there often and from there began traveling and speaking at various churches and groups throughout Nevada, California, and Tennessee. During this time, I also reconnected with the Sacramento Prayer House. I had often gone there while I was still attending Trinity. When I would go to Sacramento to visit Mom, I would also visit the Sacramento Prayer House. Shortly after I reconnected, Oren and Bernice Burkett announced a ministry trip to Baja. They would be taking food, bibles, building materials, church furnishings, clothes, and medical supplies to hospitals, churches and orphanages. I signed up to go.

A couple of months later we went in an old school bus loaded with supplies for the various needs. It was incredible to be able to help supply the needs of so many. On the way back I was asked what I thought of the trip. I said that it was great—but I wanted more. I wanted to see people come to Christ. I wanted to see people healed, transformed, and made whole. My heart yearned for souls, so I told them that I would really like to have crusades down there. They wanted to know where. I felt like we should start in San Ignacio. It so happened that we were only an hour away, so the driver stopped there. I went in and shared my vision with a local pastor. We were both very excited. San Ignacio would become the first of many. I made several trips down to various towns in Baja meeting with local pastors to plan the crusades.

San Ignacio was a town of about 900 people. Probably two to three hundred came to the crusade, including the local mayor. Many were saved and healed. We had a wonderful team from Lodi and the Sacramento Prayer House. They prayed for individuals, and the local pastors supplied us with translators.

White Trash

Mexico Leadership Team, 1989

The local pastors were exuberant and supportive of one another. They each wanted us to come to their towns and hold crusades. From San Ignacio we went to Vizcaino, an Indian farming community just north, then to Guerro Negro and El Rosario. Later we would go back down to Mulege, Ciudad Constitucion, La Paz, and Cabo San Lucas. Then a pastor asked me to go over to Obregon, and while there I also went and spoke in a women's prison. We held the crusades in churches and open-air meetings, in fields and city plazas. People continued to get saved and healed. A lady was healed of lupus in Guerro Negro; her doctor said that it was a miracle. These beautiful people were as flowers in my desert. The doors had flung open wide. I loved it. I loved the crusades, I loved the team, and I loved the people of Mexico. Then, as quickly as they had opened, the doors were shut. Steve didn't want me going to Mexico anymore. Unannounced, he had moved back to Wells while I was on a three-week trip to

Mexico. I was devastated, but it was already a done deal. I determined that by the grace of God, I would make the best of the situation.

While evangelizing in Nevada, I had filled the pulpit at the Community Presbyterian Church in Wells several times. So when we moved back to Wells, we attended it and the Episcopal Church. The pastor of the Presbyterian Church and his wife were moving back to California and wanted us to fill the pulpit, so we did. That was in 1991. Steve is still filling the pulpit there and has been considered their pastor now for more than twenty years. The Episcopal Church was also without a priest, and before long, the Bishop of Nevada had asked Steve to go to Idaho for three years of training so he could become a local priest. At the same time, I felt that God wanted me to go to Fuller Seminary in Pasadena. An interesting aspect of our marriage is that it has always been centered on ministry. We have helped each other to fulfill the call of God. Much of the time we have had separate ministries, but there have also been times when we have ministered together. It has been a blessing for us both.

At that time, our plans were that I could become a Presbyterian pastor and Steve an Episcopal priest. However, the plan wasn't without its problems. Steve would be able to continue his work at the Conservation Camp and go to school in Idaho on weekends and during his vacation time in the summer. I, on the other hand, would first have to be accepted as one called to ministry by the Presbyterians. I was. Then I had to be accepted into Fuller in order to get a Masters of Divinity, a degree that both the Presbyterians and the Episcopalians required before they would be willing to ordain me. This meant not only did I have to apply, be accepted and jump through all the hoops the denomination required, which were many, but I also had to complete my bachelor's degree. I had more than enough units for my bachelor's. However, I lacked one social science, so I agreed to take an anthropology class during the summer and was granted the bachelor's degree. I was accepted! Thank God!

Of course, there was the issue of how this all would be funded. Three years of seminary would be costly. We had a little in savings, but not enough to get all the way through. Bless his heart, Steve was willing to sell his airplane, but he was not willing to go into debt. We decided that I would go as far as I could. So we both went, and we both studied. However, I had no peace about becoming a Presbyterian minister, so I decided that I should speak with Bishop Zabriskie of Nevada. He was excited about me becoming an Episcopal priest, so he flew to California and met me in Glendale. He wanted me to come on board with them. I switched to the Episcopal Church and continued my studies. The Bishop asked about my marriages. When I told him, he didn't have any issues with my past. The Episcopal Church at large was a lot more concerned about my Pentecostal experiences than they were about how many times I had been married.

Midway through seminary, Steve and I ran out of money. Steve called and said that I would have to quit at the end of the quarter. I agreed, but I also prayed. A few weeks later, as I was working on one of my class reports, the phone rang. It was a call from New York, a couple who were excited about Steve and me becoming Episcopal priests in rural Nevada wanted to pay the rest of my tuition and housing. They also wanted to send money for clergy vestments. I was grateful, humbled, and overwhelmed. How generous! What an incredible answer to prayer! I'm not sure that they even knew our circumstances.

While I was at Fuller, I interned at Saint Jude's, a Charismatic Episcopal Church in Burbank. It was a wonderful church, and it was great working with Father Flynn. I learned a lot about intercession and inner healing which I needed desperately, especially in the area of rejection. Even with the mention of the word rejection, tears would fill my eyes. I needed to be healed.

When the Holy Spirit works in my life, it seems as though a magnifying glass is placed on a particular area. This time it was in the area of rejection. Every time I turned around, it felt as if I was being rejected. During that time of healing, I had a dream that took me back to the point of my conception. It was so real. Mom was with Uncle Wilbur, my dad's brother. They both had been drinking, and Mom was tipsy. They ended up having an affair, and I was conceived in that affair. When I woke up, I was devastated. It felt like my heart was bleeding inside. My pain was so deep.

Uncle Wilbur had tried to tell me one time when I was a teenager, but I had refused to listen. I didn't think much of Dad, but I couldn't stand Uncle Wilbur. He seemed so depraved, so evil. I certainly didn't want him to be my dad.

Now I find out that, not only was I a bastard child, I was this depraved man's bastard child. Why hadn't Mom told me? My pain wouldn't go away. For three days, my heart literally felt like it was bleeding. Pain and shame flooded me. I knew that talking to Mom wasn't a good idea when I was in so much pain. I finally went to an Episcopal priest who prayed with me. That started a flood of healings.

I don't know how God healed my broken heart, but He did. I felt waves of the love of my heavenly Father come over my being. He let me know that He was my Father and He loved me. It was wonderful. God did such a deep healing from rejection in my childhood and from my own failed marriages. I also repented for doing the same thing as my mom had done. I hadn't been drinking, and I justified the relationship, by thinking that "I was in love." Nevertheless one of my own children was the result of an affair. I was so sorry, and I cried out for forgiveness. God assured me of His forgiveness. God forgave me. However, it was not nearly so easy for me to forgive me. Later the Lord spoke to me concerning my refusal to forgive myself. If He had forgiven me, who did I think I was not to forgive myself? God wanted me to forgive everyone, even myself. Finally with His help, I was able to do that. Forgiveness was setting me free. During this time of healing, God put a little song in my heart.

> *"He saw me broken, discarded, lonely and used. And He said, 'I'll pick up the pieces and make you brand new'. My Jesus, my Jesus, He died for me. My Jesus, my Jesus, He set me free. He loved me; He healed me; He made me brand new. My Jesus, Jesus, He set me free."*

At Saint Jude's, not only was I being ministered to, but I was also being set free to move in the gifts of the Spirit and minister to others. I especially moved with the gifts of prophecy[i] and inner healing.

This Episcopal connection felt comfortable and right because Saint Luke's Episcopal Church was where I first attended and taught with Patty. That had been during the Charismatic Renewal of the 1970's. Sad to say, I would never find another Episcopal church like Saint Jude's Burbank. Most were not nearly so free. It is true that, *where the Spirit of the Lord is, there is liberty*[ii].

The Dixie Cup

In the fall of 1994, my bishop wanted me to move from Pasadena to Berkeley in order to attend Christ Divinity School of the Pacific (CDSP), an Episcopal Seminary. At CDSP, my tiny graduating class was divided—half were very liberal[iii], the other half was moderate or conservative. I was a Spirit-filled Christian from rural Nevada—that's ultra conservative! My last year in seminary would prove to be a very challenging year, partly because of this, but mainly because of my brother.

As you might say about an abused horse, Arlin "had been rode hard and put away wet." Arlin had partied hearty, and it had taken a toll on his health. He had spent time in both Folsom Prison and in San Quentin, mainly for drug-related crimes. Once he was picked up by the police with 200 pounds of marijuana in his car. Another time he had shot someone in the knee over something to do with a drug deal gone wrong.

During the January break of my last year of seminary, Mom had called and wanted me to go with her to Southern California to visit Arlin in the hospital. He was dying of a lung disease called COPD (chronic obstructive pulmonary disease). It was painful to watch.

Mom didn't want me to share my faith with him for fear that he would get upset. Shortly after we arrived, Arlin went into a coma, and Mom was in the room almost all of the time. Finally, she left and was going to be gone for a while. The curtain was pulled between Arlin and the bed next to him. I started talking to him about Jesus and eternity.

There was a Dixie cup filled with water on the bed stand next to him. I told him that I didn't know if he could hear me or not, but I was going to baptize him. When I said that, he moved his head about three inches in my direction—even though he was still in a coma. It felt like he was trying to let me know that he wanted to be baptized. For me, Arlin's token response was a sign of hope. Hope that Arlin wanted to be baptized, hope that he wanted to accept Jesus, and hope that Arlin was making things right with God. After a short prayer, I baptized him in the name of the Father, the Son, and the Holy Spirit, sprinkling him with the water from the Dixie cup.

Mom returned to the room a few moments later. I said nothing to her, but my heart was rejoicing. Arlin died shortly after our time together. Mom was crushed, and I mourned for much of my remaining time in seminary. We were only thirteen months apart in age, but were worlds apart in almost everything else. Most of my mourning was for what might have been. But hope displaced mourning because of Arlin's token move of three inches, and for that I'm so very thankful.

Episcopal Priest: Isn't That a Hoot?

Just as the Presbyterian Church is the official church of Scotland, likewise the Church of England is the official church of England. Queen Elizabeth is its official head, and the Bishop of Canterbury is its ecclesiastical head. When England colonized the world, they also established their churches wherever they went. Those churches now constitute what is called The Worldwide Anglican Communion. It is the third largest denomination in the world, and the Episcopal Church of the United States is part of that communion. The Episcopal Church is proud of its elite social and economic status.

When I finished seminary in 1995, I was ordained an Episcopal priest. Isn't that a hoot! The Bishop of Nevada was ordaining a poor, unpolished, little piece of *white trash*, whose heathen father had a fourth grade education, and whose heathen mother had only finished the eighth grade. Furthermore, my own life had certainly been riddled with personal failures. But here I was with two master's degrees from two different seminaries, and I was being ordained into the church that often refers to itself as the church of presidents. Isn't Jesus good to us? Doesn't God have a great sense of humor? He uses the foolish things of this world to confound the wise[iv]. Only God can do what God can do! How God had transformed me—in every way! God can open doors that no man can open. God had given me favor!

Steve finished his Idaho training, and he was also ordained an Episcopal priest in 1996. Our acceptance into the Episcopal Church was so very healing because of the rejection we both had felt when we were not accepted by the other denomination.

I worked on the Bishop's staff, overseeing a 33,000 square mile area of Northeast Nevada. I helped several struggling churches by training local priests and deacons in different towns and cities. I did the training on weekdays and Saturdays, and I spoke in a different church each Sunday.

The bishop and I had discussed the need for a resource center in Wells, so with the help of some great local citizens, we were able to raise funds through grants to build a building and to hire a director. It is still active today. Then, for over a year, I was also interim rector (the term for pastor in the Episcopal Church) for the wonderful people of St. Paul's in Elko.

Steve was in charge of the Episcopal and Presbyterian Churches in Wells while he was still working at the camp. He had always wanted to be bi-vocational and he was. During this same time, Jill Austin, who was working under Cindy Jacobs, contacted me. They were establishing a prayer network in each state and asked me to direct the Prayer Initiative for the whole state of Nevada. I was surprised because our location was remote, and because I was an Episcopal priest, but I gladly accepted the challenge. Steve and I also taught for Northeastern Nevada Community College out of Elko. We were plenty busy.

Round-Up of Children

All of the boys were in the military at the same time: Shaun was in the Navy, David in the Coast Guard, Dru in the Army, and Tony, our son-in-law, was in the Air Force reserves. They have been in Germany, Hawaii, Italy, Gulf War, Afghanistan, Iraq, Mexico, China, and Africa. If we wanted to have a family gathering, it was almost like we had to go on a roundup first. Steve once said that keeping up with the kids was like drawing a large circle in the sand and putting four chipmunks in the circle and expecting them all to stay there.

The chipmunks turned out okay. Shaun is no longer in the circus or entertaining on the streets of San Francisco. He has become an on-fire Christian, has married Molly, has gotten out of the Navy, and has started a computer business. Presently, he is also co-director of the Heavenly House of Prayer in South Lake Tahoe. I live very close to Shaun and Molly and enjoy our times together.

Dru married Beth, the girl who lived next door to us in Wells; they have two girls. Jordan is in college and Fallon is in high school. Dru stayed in the army and is presently a sergeant-major. Dru divorced Beth and is remarried to Victoria; they live in Texas with their children—Jordan, Adam, and Mark. Beth and Fallon live in Oregon.

Joy Gartman

David   Shaun   Dru

When Tracy and Tony returned from Hawaii, they lived in various places in the US. In 2005, they moved to Italy, and in 2007, they relocated to Fairfield, California, less than an hour's drive from me. I love it. Tony works for the civil service, and Tracy has served as Director of Christian Education on several bases, including where they were in Italy and at Fairfield. They have three children. Sarah and Caleb are still in college, and I had the privilege of presiding over the marriage their oldest daughter, Bethany, and her husband, Nathan, while they were still living in Italy. They now have two children: Brody was born in Italy and Slade was born in Kansas. God has been so good.

David joined the Coast Guard and married KiMar, a math teacher, who was living and teaching in Elko, Nevada. They moved to Pensacola, Florida, to attend the Bible College at the Brownsville Revival. They have led ministry teams to Mexico, Africa, and within the U.S. David also ministered in China and in Central America. They were at the Brownsville Revival for eight years before moving to Mexico as missionaries. After their time in Mexico, they moved back to the states and are living in Minot, North Dakota. They are still recovering from the terrible flood of 2011. David is now a general contractor, and KiMar is working on a Masters in English.

I had the opportunity to go visit them and attend the Brownsville Revival almost every year for my study leave while David and KiMar lived in Florida. It was a double blessing. After spending time with them and after attending the revival, I would always come back refreshed. One year the Lord gave me what I call a "download" on the Book of Revelation. In 2006, after seven years of it being hidden in a spiral notebook, the Lord prompted me to get it out and write my first book, which is called *END OF DAYS: Decoding the Book of Revelation*. Who would have ever thought that I would have written a book. God is so amazing. He has plans for us even when we are in our mother's womb—long before we ever have a clue.

Joy Gartman

Pictures from Wedding in Italy:
Tracy, Caleb, Sarah, Tony

Nathan, Pastor Joy, Bethany

Fires

Steve transferred to the Division of Forestry in Las Vegas in 1999. One of the main things he did there was build road crossings and fences for desert turtles, in an effort to keep them from being totally annihilated by the traffic. He was also involved in fighting fires, plus he and his crews helped replant trees and other shrubs after fires or storms had passed.

With Steve's move to Las Vegas, I would no longer be able to cover Northeast Nevada for the Bishop, so before we left Wells, I started asking different people about positions that might be open in Las Vegas. At that time, All Saints' Episcopal Church in Las Vegas was the third largest Episcopal Church in the state of Nevada. It had almost four hundred parishioners with an average attendance of 225 per Sunday and a school of 120 students K-1st grade. They were looking for a rector. The position would start around the same time that Steve needed to relocate. Leaders in the diocese encouraged me to put my name on the list for consideration. By the grace of God, I was chosen to become their senior pastor.

The timing was perfect, so Steve and I bought a house and moved to Las Vegas. All Saints' was a real blessing in so many ways. Even though it was a larger church, it wasn't hard to maintain because their building was fairly new and seldom needed repair, and they had an exceptional staff—especially some of the volunteer retired staff. One of my deacons, John, and his wife were an incredible support and were always willing to help. Stewart was a retired Lutheran pastor who loved to teach and visit shut-ins, and we had a retired military chaplain who also helped. They both were excellent preachers. Our music was also led by volunteers. One was a Catholic monk who led the choir for the traditional services. Jim Smith moved to Las Vegas shortly after I arrived. He had led contemporary music back east, so his skills were a perfect match for our newly-formed contemporary service. He was always pleasant and helpful. My administrative assistant, the school principal and many more teachers and leaders were so outstanding. What an asset!

Steve chose to take a sabbatical from ministry while we were in Las Vegas so that he could concentrate on his new responsibilities at work. Much of our marriage has been centered on ministry. Sometimes we have had separate ministries and sometimes when we have ministered together. It has been a blessing for us both. In Las Vegas, I would stand alone in ministry. This was okay because God had supplied me with such a wonderful team.

Steve and I were still enjoying and adjusting to our new location and responsibilities when we experienced the 9-11 attacks. The initial shock of the attack within our own country and our sudden awareness of our country's vulnerability caused the churches to be full for a few weeks.

One of my joys at All Saints was doing Wednesday chapel for the school. I had taught kindergarten and first grade while in

Hawaii, so doing the chapel for that age group was fun and reminiscent of that time. We had a memorial service for the first graders and kindergarteners after the 9-11 attack, which was televised on the evening news in Las Vegas. I had the children bring something from home that reminded them of the event so they could place it on the memorial. Some brought little toy fire trucks and planes, others flowers, little flags, candles, and other commemorative items. They were all so serious and precious during the prayer time. It was a very touching event.

Some in the church had scheduled an Oktoberfest for the last weekend of September. The United States and the whole world were in shock and mourning. International games and events were being canceled, and memorial services were happening all over the world. It seemed totally inappropriate to have a time of celebration when so many were grieving, so I canceled the Oktoberfest. What a hornets' nest that stirred up! It was only a tiny percentage, some ten to twelve of the church's old guard, but they were furious. That little group of people was set on making my life miserable from that point forward—and they did! But the other members were very healthy spiritually, and we were growing.

We did the Alpha Course, and through that many were getting saved, healed, and filled with the Holy Spirit. It was a blessed time for the church as a whole. Margaret was in the final stage of cancer when her doctor suggested that she discontinue her treatment so that she could add as much quality as possible to her remaining days. Her husband, Robert, had been attending the Alpha Course when, in one of the sessions, our attention was turned toward healing. Robert went home and told Margaret. I was pleased when they both came into my office for prayer. Margaret shares her own story in the next chapter. She was completely healed and is well to this day. Praise the Lord! Jesus still heals!

Margaret's Testimony

"When Joy Gartman told me in all seriousness that God could heal my cancer, I would have rolled my eyes if I hadn't been raised in a polite household. I had come to see Joy in hopes of getting my spiritual ducks in a row. I just couldn't make peace with the idea that I was dying. I was awake every night, unable to accept that this was my fate.

It's not that I doubted the diagnosis. The breast tumor had grown to the size of a golf ball and spread into my lymph nodes by the time the doctors figured out it was cancer and not a benign cyst. I'd been through two surgeries, the second one - the dreaded mastectomy - because the lumpectomy did not get all the cancer. Next came chemotherapy. Every three weeks I'd get plugged in to IV's containing the poison that would leave me nauseated and bald. Then there were blood tests. My blood counts plummeted. I'd get daily injections in my belly to stimulate my bone marrow to make blood cells. My bones throbbed like I had the flu.

I was too weak and tired to work, and unable to focus on TV or reading, so monitoring my lab tests became my pastime. I had a medical background, and I poured over my lab tests the way a sports enthusiast pours over baseball stats. The print outs showed what the normal range was and "flagged" each value that was either high or low. I became fascinated with the way my blood counts would plummet in the days following a chemo session. Red blood count down. Down again. And again. Doctor says any lower and I'll need a transfusion. White count down. Stay indoors and away from other people and possible germs. Doctor says no fresh fruits for fear they might harbor a bacteria or mold my body would be unable to fight. I diligently watched my lab print outs. How many new white cells were my bones generating. . . ?

After a few weeks, two new tests suddenly appeared on my printout: the CA 27-29 and the CEA. Both were flagged way above normal. I had no idea what these tests were so I called my doctor's nurse. She told me these were tests for a protein that would appear in my blood if I had a tumor growing, a sign that the cancer has spread, or in medical terms, metastasized. I knew that once a cancer metastasizes, what lies ahead for the patient is a miserable fight - just to delay the inevitable. Alarmed I asked, "Do I have a tumor growing?" She said she didn't know and suggested I speak with my doctor.

My doctor told me not to be alarmed, these tests sometimes spike for no apparent reason. The only reason to be alarmed is if these tests show an upward trend. I calmed down and waited for the next results. The CA 27-29 and CEA went higher. Uneasy, I waited another week for the next test. Higher. Uneasiness turned to anxiety. Another test. Higher still. Beyond anxiety and almost in a panic, I waited for the next test. Even higher. About this time tests showed that my liver enzymes were haywire. I knew that the liver is one of the places breast cancer is likely to spread.

Frantic, I scheduled an appointment to see my doctor. "Is the chemo helping at all?" I asked.

She said she didn't know, and wrote an order for repeat CAT scans and bone scans to see where the cancer might be spreading. She said we would then evaluate and determine what treatment, if any, to proceed with. I made my appointment with the radiologist.

It was about this time I arrived at All Saints Church office pale, bald and exhausted. I figured a priest would be equipped to guide me through this anxiety. If this church stuff didn't work, I reasoned, next I'd try yoga. . . or meditation of some kind.

I hadn't visited an Episcopal Church in years, although I'd been raised in the church. My grandfather was a priest. My grandmother was the "church matriarch." My mother played the organ. And my brother and I fidgeted in the front pew next to Grandma every Sunday throughout our childhoods. But as I entered my teens, I began to question things that didn't make sense to me. Sunday worship had become empty—just "going through the motions." When I was old enough to make my own decisions, I decided that sleeping late on Sunday mornings was a much better use of my time. And that's exactly what I did every Sunday morning for the next 20 years.

It took cancer and the coaxing of my husband, Bob, to get me to agree to see Joy Gartman at the church. What I didn't realize was that Bob was experiencing a spiritual crisis of his own triggered by all the bad-news-on-top-of-bad-news we were getting.

So there I sat, facing Joy Gartman for the first time, fully expecting to get instruction on how to die. I couldn't have been more surprised when she told me that God could heal me.

Episcopalians don't believe that stuff, I thought. . . do they? I mean, I believed in God, and even believed in Jesus to some degree. But faith healing? That was just a ridiculous hoax performed on TV by a shouting, sweaty evangelist in a white linen suit, just before he asked for the audience to send in money.

Joy picked up a well worn and dog-eared Bible. In her hands this Bible seemed to fall open on its own to scripture after scripture detailing the healings performed by Jesus. She read to me as though she was presenting absolute evidence that I could be healed too. Sure, I told myself, Jesus healed people who were actually with him over 2000 years ago. But what's that got to do with me? These are modern times.

Joy anointed me with oil and prayed with us. Then she gave me a "prescription." She said to pray every day and read the Gospel of John. At this point I spoke up. "Isn't it unreasonable for me to expect God, the mighty Creator of the Universe, to be bothered with a little flea like me?" Joy explained that God wants a relationship with each of us and welcomes our prayers.

I left Joy's office doubtful. The next morning, I decided to give her "prescription" a shot. After all, I reasoned, what did I have to lose?

Bob and I dusted off the Bible we had on our book shelf, and read to each other from the Gospel of John. It was the first time I had ever read a Gospel in its entirely. During Sunday worship in the Episcopal Church, only small excerpts from the Bible are read. The last time I had tried to seriously read the Bible had been when I was a little girl. We had a King James Bible in our household, with all the "thee's" and "thou's", which made it a rather difficult read, especially for a child. I recall starting with Genesis (the beginning I reasoned) and struggling forward. When I came to page after page of who begot whom, I finally gave up. This was the last time I had attempted to read the Bible.

It took very little time for Bob and me to finish the Gospel of John and I was amazed at how brief and to the point it was. Afterwards, on my own, I paged back to the Gospel of Mathew and read the entire New Testament for the first time. Then I started over again, slowly and thoughtfully.

The praying part of Joy's prescription really had me stumped. I could certainly recite the Lord's Prayer, but that seemed like repeating empty words. If I wasn't reciting the Lord's Prayer, what worthwhile thing could I possibly say to God? I pictured myself sitting on God's lap, like a greedy little girl asking Santa for the latest toy I'd seen on TV. How infantile! In this case I'd be asking for healing. But since God already knows everything that is in our hearts, what is the point of praying anyway?

But I had decided to give Joy's prescription a serious effort, so the following morning went into the bedroom, closed the door and kneeled by the bed as I had when a child. It had been decades since I'd done this and my much-older knees complained on the hardwood floors. I placed a pillow on the floor and kneeled on that. Much better. I started with the Lord's Prayer, one line at a time. I quietly contemplated the meaning of each line, and then "sent" it to God. Next I asked God to heal me. Mostly I stayed quiet. My entire prayer session lasted an hour or so, and I emerged feeling calm and refreshed, and even somewhat hopeful for the first time since I had been diagnosed.

That evening I did the same thing again. And the next morning. And the next evening. My prayer began to evolve. I always began slowly and thoughtfully with the Lord's Prayer. But then I started to ask for God's guidance so that I could make the good choices for my health.

In the meantime, I went for my repeat CAT scan and bone scans. I prayed as the x-ray machines passed over me. I returned home, hopeful, but not really optimistic.

I continued reading the Bible and praying. Bob and I began attending services at All Saints. Joy's sermons were a refreshing and joyful expression of God's love. I looked forward to our private meetings with her. The best phrase I can think of to describe Joy Gartman is quietly powerful. Her sincerity and absolute belief are contagious. Her calm manner sooths. On our drive home one afternoon, I turned to Bob and said, "Joy is the real thing." I quietly sent a prayer of thanks to God for placing Joy in our lives.

A few days after the repeat CAT scan, I called the radiology office to see if my scans had been read by the doctors. I was too impatient to wait for my appointment to hear the results. Yes, the scans were read and my report completed. The receptionist told me I could come by the office to pick up the report. That afternoon, we sat in the waiting room waiting for the print out of the report. Finally they called me to the desk and handed me an envelope with my name on it. I returned to my seat beside Bob and tore opened the envelope. I skimmed to the summary at the bottom. The results said "normal" . . . no evidence of metastasis.

I burst into tears of happiness. An elderly lady seated down the row from us looked over, concerned. Through my tears I told her it was good news. She smiled, reached in her purse, and handed me one of those small evangelism pamphlets with the headline that read, "God loves you."

I returned to my oncologist later that week. She had a copy of the report, which she went over with me. She was plainly surprised by the results and called the radiologists to ask them to obtain my first CAT scan to do a side by side comparison. I can't exactly say why, but I was calmly confident that they would find nothing (and they did not). We decided to go forward with the remainder of my chemotherapy and radiation.

My next blood test showed the CA27-29 and CEA moving downward, toward the normal range. The test after that showed lower still. Finally, my results showed normal, and have stayed that way ever since. It's been 12 years now.

In the years since we first encountered Joy Gartman, Bob and I have become Healing Touch practitioners and instructors. This is a form of soaking prayer and laying on of hands. With divine guidance, Bob created www.Healing Scripture.com, a website which has a following of thousands from around the world. The website details the healings of Jesus, and has testimonials and a powerful prayer chain, with miraculous impact for many. We are active with our local church. We pray every day. And we still thank God for placing Joy Gartman in our lives."

Margaret's healing was such a miracle. What an encouragement to us all. However, shortly after Margaret's healing everything switched. I was diagnosed with lung cancer. Now Bob and

Margaret were faithfully praying for me. For weeks, they came to my house to pray soaking prayers with the laying on of hands. And God heard their prayers! Jesus healed me!

Vision of Revival

Right after Margaret's healing and the events of 911, I had a vivid dream about war and revival. War was on the minds of almost everyone. We were wondering whether or not we would go to war, and if we did, with what nation. This dream was early 2002, just a few months before the United States declared war on Iraq.

The Lord Jesus came to me on a white horse. I got on the horse with him, and we both rode it back into heaven. After being in heaven for a while, we came back down to earth just northeast of Iraq. We were in what seemed to be Iran, looking toward Baghdad, viewing the initial blitz. It was so real that when I later saw it on the news, I wept. It was exactly what I had seen in the dream. We rode the horse through the streets of Baghdad, viewing the carnage. The look on the Lord's face was very somber.

The scene shifted. The Lord and I were suddenly at a large assembly room in Jerusalem. There were many people from various nations. I realized that the people were there because there was going to be a worldwide revival. I also knew that there was going to be a revival in Israel. The Lord Jesus Himself was going to initiate that revival. While I was lost in thought about the revivals, particularly about revival in the United States, I was handed a scepter its diameter was a little larger than a hand-held microphone and about three feet long. The scepter had lots of fire and sparks flying off the end of it.

The scenes changed again. I was back in the United States, somewhere on the east coast. I was being directed to go to certain towns. As the scepter touched the towns, a fire would appear in that town. The first place with a fire seemed to be near a river in North or South Carolina. There were a few little fires in other towns all across the US. I no longer remember all of the places. One seemed to be near the panhandle of Texas. A few were in the Midwest and the North. There were two very small sparkling fires in Las Vegas and in the Sparks/Reno. Then I saw a couple of fires in Washington State near the Canadian border. As I traveled south, the number of fires increased, and in southern Oregon, both the frequency and intensity of the fires increased. When I entered into California, I found myself by the ocean, touching the scepter into the Pacific Ocean. I had an inward knowing that revival would hit some of the coastal towns. In the center of Northern California, there were lots of fires, more than I had seen anywhere. There were fewer fires as I traveled toward the middle of the state, and fewer still in Southern California. If I remember correctly, there was one in Riverside. I asked the Lord why the fire and sparkles on the end of the scepter. Jesus spoke to my spirit, "They are the Fire and the Glory." Since then I have had many other dreams and visions, and several of them have been in connection with revival.

The reason for mentioning this dream about the scepter in this book is that this dream indicated to me that there would be a shift in the direction of my ministry, and in fact, within the last few years, my desires have changed. There has been less desire for serving as a pastor, and more desire to serve as an evangelist or revivalist. I have always been an intercessor.

We need another mighty move of God. People need to be saved, healed, and set free. Christians need to be transformed into the likeness of Jesus. The world needs once again to experience miracles and the other supernatural manifestations that are frequently associated with revivals and reformations. I am not alone in these desires.

Many others have hungered for souls, and some have prophesied of a mighty move of God. Countless unknown Christians worldwide are praying—interceding for revival. This movement is more than the ambitions of man. It has been generated from the heart of Father God Himself. God has a master plan. He has given each of us certain gifts, abilities and desires to fulfill His plan to bring about a worldwide harvest. The Spirit of God wants to hover over humankind again and give light for darkness, wholeness for brokenness, victory for defeat, order for chaos, and repentance and transformation for us all.

The Holy Spirit was redirecting my life. Part of this change of direction would include relocating to Northern California. God's plans are so much bigger than we can think or imagine.

Beauty for Ashes

While Steve was nearing retirement from the Nevada Department of Forestry, Mom was aging in Sacramento. I wanted to be closer to her during her final years. There was an opening for a senior pastor at a small Episcopal Church in Marysville, California, just fifty minutes north of Mom. Since Steve hated big cities and California, this smaller community would be much more pleasing to him.

The church only had a little over seventy members, but I felt that God wanted me to submit my name. I did, and was called to be their senior pastor starting in June of 2002. The Bishop called Steve to be my assistant after he retired from Nevada in January 2003. St. John's was pleased and so were we!

The church building had been neglected for many years, and it needed a lot of work. The people were excited and generous as we raised funds for a major overhaul. One of the renovations was with a large room that had been called

Joy at Saint John's 2002

Ghirardelli Hall (donated by the Ghirardelli family). That room went through a beautiful transformation. People were eager to help, and many even wanted to buy stain glass windows. It was lovely in every sense of the word. We started a contemporary service in the hall and referred to it as Christ's Chapel. Several new families joined us. We did the Alpha Course as I had done in Las Vegas. Seventy plus people signed up to attend. It was great, and there was a lot of excitement. Again people were getting saved, filled with the Holy Spirit and healed. Kelly Bronson and her husband, James, were one of the new couples attending Christ Chapel. The following is part of her testimony from 2005.

"Ten years prior I was diagnosed with hepatitis C and psoriases of the liver. Back then I didn't care if I lived or died, until God gave me my husband, James, and brought pastors Steve and Joy into my life. Joy had a class on hearing God. The first time I listened, God spoke to me and said. 'Do the treatments my child and I will carry you through.' So I spoke to Pastor Joy and told her that I felt that I needed to be obedient. She agreed and said, 'Let's pray.' So we did.

"I went to the doctor, and they ran the tests. When the test came back they told me that the disease had gone too far and they didn't want to do the treatments. I cried and begged them to start them. Finally they agreed to them, even though they didn't think that they would do any good. I told Pastor Joy what the doctors had said. Again she wanted to pray. We prayed. The congregation prayed, and Brad Taylor prayed, 'Lord let the doctors be *baffled*.' Three months into my treatment they took another blood test. When it came back they called me into the office. They said, 'You *baffle* us; your blood work came back undetectable.' I have now been undetectable for over seven years. God is a truthful God!"

All was wonderful at Saint John's and Christ's Chapel for a while, until a few liberals from Saint John's, who were connected with the diocese, started attacking those in the church who were more conservative, including Steve, me and most all of those who were attending Christ's Chapel, the newly formed contemporary service. The liberal contingent formed a group, and they started writing a "newsletter" called "Friends of St. John's." That group came against about half of the church. The church became polarized. People who had been friends for years were now on opposite sides. The bishop was liberal and was encouraging the ones who had been writing the newsletters. It was a really difficult situation for a church to endure. As a leader, it was hard not to be discouraged. One day during a particularly difficult siege a little song popped in to my mind.

> "We don't have to stay stuck.
> We can move from this rut.
> We can trust in the Lord as we forward go.
> The blues will stay behind us,
> The guilt, the pain, the shame
> We can trust in our Jesus,
> We can trust his Holy Name."

I went around softly singing this a lot. Sometimes I would sing *I don't have to stay stuck* instead of *we don't have to stay stuck*.... This little jingle brought me hope. And it would end up being more prophetic than I could have ever imaged.

On top of all of this, or maybe because of it, in early 2004, I was diagnosed with breast cancer, and had to have a biopsy. When the doctor did the biopsy, he cut through the center of the cancer. I was devastated because this cut could cause the cancer to spread. One of the foreign medical technicians had done an ultrasound instead of a mammogram. When they rolled me in for the operation, I was still somewhat conscious and heard the doctor complain that he didn't know how to read ultrasounds for surgery. After surgery, the report showed that half of the cancer was still there, so I went to San Francisco for more tests and surgeries. After they had done another surgery, they found that there were also early signs of cancer in the other breast. The only good thing in all of this was that I was forced to go somewhere else where they would examine me more extensively. I had a total of four surgeries, including a double mastectomy. By that time I was also being treated for high blood pressure.

I recovered quickly from the whole cancer ordeal, but in 2006, I fell while cleaning some spilled coke off the back cement steps of the church. I fractured my T-5 vertebrae. It was very painful and required a back brace for a couple of years, until I was healed. That happened when two young women prayed for me at Bethel Church in Redding, California. I felt heat go through my back under the brace. The next morning the pain was gone. Thank you Jesus!

Towards the end of 2007, my heartbeat slowed down to 32 beats per minute, and then no heart beat could be detected. I ended up in the hospital again, and in January of 2008, I had to have a pacemaker implanted. I continued to pastor the church through these times, but thank God for Steve. He truly stepped in to help during this most critical period, even though he was still a part-time pastor in Wells.

The conflict in the church between liberals and conservatives raged on. The members who were being criticized came to me and begged me to leave St. John's Marysville and start an Anglican Church across the river in Yuba City. Sylvia, whose family had been Episcopalians for thirteen generations, all the way back to Jamestown, asked me what we would need to do to start a new church. My long list included having an Anglican covering and a place to meet. She urged me to go with her to look for a place. She felt that we should drive around right then and look. We had gone no more than three blocks from where we were having lunch when we both spotted the storefront. She got the number and was going to call.

Starting a new church was about the last thing Steve and I wanted to do, but we couldn't stand by or leave, as we had planned. We were unwilling to see sincere, Christ-believing Christians abandoned at such a time. The bishop was liberal and had joined the side of the liberal agitators.

The majority of the Worldwide Anglican Communion is conservative, especially in Asia, Africa, and South America, and they have been extremely supportive of the Anglicans who left the Episcopal Church USA. Steve and I were both accepted into the dioceses of Bolivia and I into the Anglican Church of Kenya. Since the split, an Anglican Communion has been formed in North America, and Trinity Anglican Church of Yuba City is a member of that communion.

The parishioners who left St. John's to form Trinity Church truly took the higher road. They prayed for and wished the others the best. They didn't fight back, even though they were extremely hurt. They didn't demand their rights, even though they felt the loss of their church home, a beautiful building with stained glass windows, bell tower, and so many memories. It had been like the end of a bitter marriage. However, they left with honor, and they left with grace in their desire to follow Jesus, no matter the cost. I felt like a proud parent because of their Christ-like behavior. They built beauty on the ashes of what had been and what might have been.

At our first service on August 27, 2006, the lectionary reading for that Sunday "happened" to be about how the Lord had parted the waters for Moses when the children of Israel left Egypt on their way to the Promised Land. We had just crossed the river between Marysville and Yuba City to enter into our new church start. Remember the little song? *"We don't have to stay stuck"* Well we didn't stay stuck; we had moved on, and God provided everything we needed: building, chairs, leaders, piano, altar, pulpit—everything—even bagpipes to play Amazing Grace. Plus, that first Sunday, we celebrated eight baptisms! These were people who had joined the newly-formed contemporary service at St. John's in Christ's Chapel. Most of them were included among those who had been under attack. What a celebration! God continued to work mightily in our midst. Many were healed, saved, and filled with the Holy Spirit.

Kelly had another miraculous healing in 2007. She had been diagnosed with colon cancer and had to have surgery. Steve and I were already at the hospital praying when we were told that while the doctor was removing the cancer, her appendix burst. Many were praying. Kelly later said, "I was able to feel Pastor Joy's and Steve's prayers. When the biopsy came back, my doctor said I was a miracle. I thank God for His love for me and the faith He has given me." That was more than five years ago and Kelly is still cancer free.

Steve and I had the pleasure of serving Trinity Church until our retirement became official on March 10, 2012. We were so blessed when those wonderful people gave us an awesome farewell party. The people of that church must be the best cooks in northern California. They are the only people I know that consistently have *five-star* potlucks. That final potluck was certainly no exception. After ten years as pastor of these faithful ones, the baton has now been passed. Father Victor has been called and anointed as their new priest from the newly formed Anglican Church of North America. We really feel good about Father Victor, his wife and the future of Trinity Church. *The gates of hell will not prevail*[v] over God's plans and purposes.

Joy Gartman

Trinity 3-10-2010 – Steve, Joy & Sylvia

Amazing Grace

After I accepted the call to St. John's, Marysville and moved to Yuba City, I so enjoyed being around Mom. She had quit drinking and had mellowed a lot over the years. She was a wonderful grandma, aunt, friend, and rescuer. She had a kindness that especially extended to the down-and-outers and to my cousins. I saw something in her latter years that may have helped explain our relationship. Mom needed to be needed and wanted to be wanted—and she was! She was needed by many. But, for some reason, I had seldom felt needy, even when I was in dire need. It never occurred to me that Mom or anyone else might actually want to help. Other than asking Dad to rescue me from Hal, I don't remember asking anyone else for help, except a couple of times I asked for a loan, which was quickly paid back. However, even though I don't remember asking them, people did help. Maybe I was too independent for my own good. Mom had often helped Arlin, but Mom, too, seldom asked for help for herself. She was much more comfortable being a helper, rather than a help-ee.

Mom was helping others in many ways. She was sending care packages to prisons, but instead of sending them to Arlin, now she was sending them to her nephews. It seemed like they filled part of that huge empty space left in Mom's life after Arlin died. She didn't have a lot, but she used her widow's mite to give to those in need. She would go to garage sales and buy clothes and blankets for my other cousins and their children. Often I felt that her actions were more Christ-like than most of us who professed Christianity. Many of the people Mom helped were children of Uncle Harl. Uncle Harl was the baby boy who had gone with Mom to live with their aunt and uncle after her mother died. There had always been a special bond between them. She was also a great friend to those in trouble. She was one who would listen without judging. She loved them all and they loved her! Mom had become close friends with Uncle Harl's oldest daughter, Susan. Susan had also become a Christian and was able to lead her father to the Lord before he died.

Mom had been strong, independent, and extremely healthy her whole life. But in the last few years, she had some problems with her health that sent her to the hospital for a week or so. It was in July of 2008, when David and KiMar had come up from Mexico, and I had flown into Mobile. We all met and drove down to Lakeland, Florida for a revival. We were driving back up to Alabama to meet with Steve, his brother, Terry, and his stepmother, Jean, when we got a call from Shaun and Molly reporting that Mom was in the hospital. She was not expected to live very long. Her lung was filled with fluid and cancer. Before, when she had been critically ill, we had all prayed for Mom's healing, and she had been miraculously healed each time. However, this time was different, for I knew in my spirit that it was her time to go. I prayed for God to show His mercy and save her. I also told the

Lord that I wanted to know; I didn't want her to sneak into heaven without us knowing that she was saved.

Steve and I flew back to Sacramento at the end of July 2008, and David was also able to come to help us with Mom. The doctors said that Mom could be released from the hospital if someone could take care of her at home. Steve could minister at the church while I took care of her. David could help on either end, at the church or at Mom's. Molly was able to make all the contacts for hospice. Just one big snare! Mom didn't want me to be her caregiver. Why? I was a Christian. Even though I had never witnessed to her in the over thirty-five years since I had been saved, she still wasn't comfortable with me and my faith. She wanted a non-Christian friend of my cousin to take care of her. It just so happened that Mom's choice of caregivers had another commitment, and I was the only one left to care for her. She would have to settle for me. With Molly's help, we *were* able to get hospice care right away because Mom was really failing fast.

Even though Mom had softened through the years, she remained unsaved. She pretended to the kids that she was saved in order to please them and to keep them from witnessing to her. My first clue that she was pretending to be a Christian was at Arlin's death in 1995. She loved Arlin more than any other living being and only wanted his best. So, when she didn't want me to witness to him when he was dying, I knew that she didn't believe. This time, I urged the kids to mainly pray for her salvation. We were all putting her on every prayer list we knew, asking everyone to pray that she be saved. Mom was 89 years old at that time. In her life, there were several times when she was *almost* saved, but each time something happened, and for some reason she rejected the Spirit. It seemed that after every *almost saved, but not quite saved* incident, her heart became harder.

There had been a couple of supernatural events that had given me hope for Mom's salvation. First, there was the dream that she had about falling into heaven. Her dream was shortly after her sister Lola and her baby had died. Mom's mother had already died a couple of years earlier, while giving birth to Uncle Harl. At the time of her dream, Mom was wondering if they were in heaven. Mom described her dream to me in some detail before I became a Christian. She told me about seeing lots of people she knew who had already died. She saw a community with houses and people and even animals and very green grass. She said she saw both her mother and sister. It was all so very interesting. But to me, the most intriguing part of her dream was that Mom had seen herself *falling* into heaven. In her later years, I often reflected on that dream. After I became a Christian, her dream became my hope! Hope that she would end up in heaven—even if she had to *fall* into it!

Second, a year or two before Mom got so sick, I told her about a vision I had of going up into heaven. There was a lot more in the dream, but I just told Mom about the part of me seeing her last husband, Tex, up there with some horses. In his lifetime, Tex had bred horses and raised appaloosas. Tex was a true horseman; he was even California state champion for ring-spearing. Ring-spearing is an ancient sport where horseback riders race around a track with the horse reins in one hand and a very long spear in the other hand. They spear and pick up little metal rings about three inches in diameter as they race. Quite honestly, I was shocked to see Tex in heaven, because at the time, I didn't know that Shaun had befriended Tex and led him to the Lord before he died. When I told Mom about this dream, she was shocked and visibly shaken. Without thinking, she blurted out, "Why, if that ornery old coot can get into heaven, so can I." Her statement was very telling. First of all, she was surprised that Tex could get into heaven. She obviously didn't know that Shaun had led him to the Lord. It also spoke of her understanding of how one gets into heaven. By her statement, she clearly thought that someone gets into heaven by being good—and she considered herself as good as, or maybe even better than Tex. However, salvation comes not by our works but by the grace of God, by repenting of sins and by accepting Jesus as Savior and Lord. I had never told Mom that Dad was saved, and since she didn't know that Arlin and Tex were saved, she had no expectation or hope of herself ever being saved.

One day just a couple of weeks after we had returned from Florida, one of the nurses helped me load Mom in the car to take her to the hospital. I thought it would help if her lung was drained, but when we got there, the doctor was certain that she was dying. He was very kind and allowed us to stay in his office until her bed was ready in the hospital. Mom was in and out of consciousness that whole day. That night, she went to heaven and she saw Uncle Avery. Avery was the oldest of her three brothers, and he had died several years before. He had been a Baptist preacher. She later told me that she must have been hallucinating. He came to her, wanting her to go with him, but she didn't trust him and wouldn't go. We don't know if she really died or had a vision, but she remained unsaved. She returned home in a few days. Thank God for Steve and David, because after she returned home, we were up with Mom every two or three hours giving her medication. She was on a hospital bed by that time, and I was sleeping on a twin bed beside her.

Then my daughter, Tracy, had a dream where she saw Mom and Arlin in heaven. I encouraged Tracy to come over and share her dream with Mom. This dream was pivotal for Mom. Tracy's dream was about Arlin in heaven, happy and dancing a little quick-step. Tracy saw him reach out his hand for Grandma like he was inviting her to dance with him, and then he pulled her into the dance. They were both giddy with happiness. At one point, Jesus joined them in their dance. Tracy noted that as she shared the dream, Mom's countenance was radiant. Tracy said that Mom's face lit up, and then she started crying and saying, "Thank you, thank you." At the time, Tracy didn't know that Arlin, like Mom, loved to dance. Arlin and I had danced when we were younger and even at parties when we were in high school.

It seems that Mom had been quite sure that Arlin had gone to hell. And… if Arlin was in hell, Mom would have chosen to be there with him. But Tracy's dream had caused Mom to wonder, *"What if Arlin wasn't in hell. What if…Arlin was in heaven instead?"* Mom seemed to be softening, and she had been so touched and encouraged by Tracy's dream. I continued to pray. Mom had taken another turn for the worse and had to be taken to a nursing home. It would be three or four days before she could come home again.

For the next couple of days after Mom came back home, Steve and I were taking shifts around the clock. She now needed pain medication every hour. David was helping by tending to things in Yuba City and taking care of the church. We were exhausted, especially me. At one point, the nurse took my blood pressure and was going to call an ambulance to have me taken to the hospital. I refused to go, but agreed to call my doctor. She called in a prescription for me, and Steve picked it up. The nurses with hospice were wonderful. They had been convinced for over a week that Mom was going to go at any time. But I knew why she couldn't go. God was making sure that we had the assurance of her eternal destiny.

Then Mom shared that she had another dream. She shared it with tears running down her face. She had seen God! She said, "He is so big," she started crying more, "and I am so small." She held her index finger and thumb very close together, as if to show me how small she was. She faintly shared a couple of other things, but I hardly heard what she was saying. My heart was leaping because I knew that she had accepted Jesus, and she had made peace with God. I also cried. "Thank you God. You didn't allow her to sneak into heaven." We all knew!

The next night Molly came over and prayed. How I appreciated that. Tracy, Tony, and the kids also came for a short visit. I decided to leave Mom for a few minutes to go with Tracy and the kids to get a bite to eat. Mom died right after we left. It was okay because we all knew. Mom had fallen into heaven!

Mom's life story tells of the incredible love, mercy and grace of our Lord Jesus Christ for just one individual. He doesn't want anyone to be eternally lost. It also shows the working of the Holy Spirit throughout a person's lifetime—even non-Christians or those standing in opposition to God.

Joy Gartman

Mom had kept Arlin's ashes since he died in 1995, so we buried them both in Sutter Cemetery at the foot of the Sutter Buttes. On their tombstone is carved AMAZING GRACE.

Alone

After Mom died, David returned to Mexico, and Steve's and my life returned to normal (whatever that means when you are still grieving). I needed to retreat somewhere by myself. Over the years I had discovered that being quiet helped me to draw near to God. In His presence, there was peace, healing and direction. That's what I needed, so I went on a four-day silent retreat. That time gave me an opportunity to replenish. I needed to be *Alone.*

My first experience with *Alone,* happened at Saint Luke's of the Mountain when I was a new Christian. A man came there with an exercise he called the "Great Experiment of John Wesley." He wanted ten people who were hungry for more of God. They would agree to do four things each week for ten weeks. First, they would meet weekly to discuss how they were doing with the exercise. Second, they agreed to give a tithe[vi] to the Lord. Third, each week, they would do a good deed for someone they didn't know personally. And finally, they agreed to set aside fifteen minutes a day for a quiet time of devotion. Out of those fifteen minutes, five minutes were to be spent reading a designated scripture for that particular day, five minutes were to be spent meditating upon the scripture, and the last five minutes were to be spent on being quiet. You were to just listen for what the Lord wanted to say to you. Well, I was certainly hungry for more of God, so I agreed to become one of the ten.

The five minutes of silence was my challenge. My mind was undisciplined and it raced. I was unable to listen. Finally, I prayed, "God if you want me to do this, you must help me." He did help. That was the first time I met the Prince of Peace. He stilled my mind and began to *talk to me*. Prior to that, the only time God could talk to me was through the scriptures or in dreams. My mind was always overactive. I did all the talking *to* God, but after the Prince of Peace came, I was also able to listen and hear the voice of God. He began speaking into my mind very softly. I also saw pictures that seemed like a heavenly movie. God taught me how to *be still and learn what it means for Him to be God*[vii]. God needed to be exalted above my mind.

Then, many years later while I was attending Fuller Seminary, I took a class on spirituality with a concentration on the spirituality of some of the saints. We read about Teresa of Avila, Saint John of the Cross, and others who had experienced God in a deeper way. I wanted that! There was a desire deep within me that wanted to experience the presence of God as never before. The class was scheduled to have the final exam. I approached the professor and asked if instead of the exam, would it be alright for me to go on a six-day silent retreat? While there I would read and report on three extra books about contemplative saints and then journal the retreat experience. He agreed to those conditions, and that became a turning point in my life. I was hooked on being alone with God, on being still and hearing the Lord's voice.

After that time, seldom would a fast consist of merely not eating food. It would also consist of the elimination of any media or communication with anyone or anything else that distracted me from the nearness of my Lord. Books could be read only if they drew me into the presence of God.

A few years ago, I began going up to Chico, California, to a Youth with a Mission (YWAM) site for a four-day silent retreat, four times a year. My intimacy with the Holy Spirit, Jesus, and Father God increased. It became clear that transformation was happening by just being in the presence of God. As the bride of my Beloved Lord Jesus, revelation knowledge expanded. Heavenly encounters, understanding mysteries and heavenly downloads all increased. These experiences became quite common. There was a drawing to be with my Beloved and to experience His great love. Inner healing came at a new depth. The eyes of my understanding were opened to see Truth as never before. Wisdom became a friend of my silence. I had opened the door of my heart and invited the Lord to come in and fellowship with me. There I discovered how much love God has for each of us and how much He wants to help us. *Behold I stand at the door and knock; if any one hear my voice and open the door, I will come into to him and sup with him, and he with me*[viii]

During these alone times, I have discovered that much of what I had done, even as a Christian leader, had been accomplished by eating from the tree of my understanding, of me-centered ways, worldly systems, and worldly wisdom; that is the tree of the knowledge of good and evil instead of the tree of life. The fruit of the tree of knowledge produced a performance mentality, a works ministry—a do, do, do, and a go, go, go, busy, busy life and ministry. My ministry had not been about doing only what the Father was doing, and it had not been about saying only what the Father was saying[ix].

Somehow, along the way of ministering, much of what I was doing had become an effort to please the Father, just as so much of my life had been trying to please Mom. Trying to earn that which has been given so freely on the cross is wasted effort. Over twenty five years of my Christian life had been spent in mainly doing. Not that it was all bad and that nothing of eternal value has remained. But, in truth, much of the works were wood, hay, and stubble[x]. So much more would have been accomplished if I had only taken time to look at the Master's plans, listen to His heartbeat and partake of His nature. My desire was to serve Him, and for that I am grateful. But my motives of service often missed the mark of the higher calling.

God is Daddy God. What truly good earthly father wants his child to feel that he needs to work for daddy's love? Father God loves—that's His nature. He first loved—long before humanity loved Him. It is Jesus who loved and died—before I was even born. His love doesn't require works. It was freely given at the foundation of the world.

What a waste, building my kingdom instead of building the Kingdom of God. God has shown me that *my* kingdom is different from His kingdom. His kingdom produces eternal benefits. His Kingdom was the one that had transformed me. In God's Kingdom the presence of Jesus changes the atmosphere. It's realized, not by my self-efforts or demands, but by my dependency upon the Spirit of God. David is a good example of one who was dependent on God. He would pray before he went to war, and then he would do only what God instructed him to do. I must abide by God's strategies instead of trying to call the shots of the Holy Spirit. Often I want to tell the Holy Spirit what He can and cannot do. I want God's kingdom, but my way.

King Saul was one ordained by Samuel, and he was of God's choosing. However when instructions were given to him through the prophet Samuel, Saul chose to disobey and do things his way. It cost him his kingdom. Spirits of pride, control and manipulation want to work through us all. Unfortunately these spirits joining with self-will only serve to delay or, even worse, derail the work of the Holy Spirit. Wow, I wonder how many times I have insisted on doing things my way? Did that possibly derail what God wanted to do in my life? Thank God that he is not through with me yet. His love continually guides, corrects and molds me in to the likeness of Jesus.

In order to become one with Him and His purposes, I must first experience the intimacy of relationship with Jesus, the Father, and the Holy Spirit. For me, that relationship is much more than flowery words or goose bump feelings. It is deep and abiding. My trust, my peace, and my love are in Him. Alone time with Jesus and the Father is where I can hear the heartbeat of the Son and learn the Master's plan. Alone time with the Father is a place to absorb His Love and receive His revelation of who He is. My prayer continues to be, "Lord, please help me to be one with You. Transform me into your image. Mold me, shape me, and use me—all for your glory, Lord."

How grateful I am for all the Lord has done! He *has* transformed me, and He is not finished. He has taken me from rags to riches, from riches to humility, from rejection to love, and from a little piece of white trash to the Bride of Christ. He truly has changed me—my ways of thinking and my want-tos. He has truly given me *beauty for ashes and joy for discouragement and failure*[xi].

I look back over my shoulder and marvel at my seventy plus years. So much! So full! It has been a grand life—so many memories. The first thirty, before Christ, seem in many ways so wasted, but then there are my children and my children's children, and their children. It seemed as though there was no direction or purpose in that part of my life, but there was. The Lord has used that to make me who I am today. Through it, He gave me grit, stamina, and determination to get up when I was down, to go on when I was tired or fed up, and to gripe less about little things. Because of my messed up life, I was so thankful when I (finally) allowed God to rescue me. Jesus has forgiven me of so much[xii].

My altercations with Mom now seem few and minor. Forgiveness and God's grace has helped me see situations differently. I have forgiven Dad and almost forgotten the bad stuff, as I have with Hal and Dale. Hal died in 2008, and Dale sent a letter to Tracy asking for her forgiveness of him. Shaun reports that not only has he repented, but he is now a Christian. Carl remains unsaved. I am still praying for his salvation. I so want to see him in heaven.

My life with Steve has been full, and our dance between Nevada and California has been interesting. I pray that some of you reading this book will also find grace, love, hope, and peace; they are really such wonderful friends. May we all find purpose for our short time on this earth, our island home. God has a plan for each of us, and it is always more wonderful than we can imagine.

In reflecting back on my life, there are regrets of things that can't be undone. I regret for not praying before my first two marriages—only God knows what would have happened differently, in both my children's lives and in my life—if I had only prayed. I regret having an affair, and I regret for not asking Jesus into my heart as a teenager, before messing up my life and the lives of my children.

But I don't regret my children. I rejoice in my children. They and their children and grandchildren have brought such love and joy into my life. I certainly don't regret that I accepted Jesus Christ as my Savior and my Lord. That was the pivotal point in my life; it is when my life became filled with purpose. I don't regret allowing God to heal me, love me, transform me, and fill me with promise.

I don't regret my *alone* time with God—it has been more than I could have ever imagined. I don't regret serving God's people. Sometimes it has been a challenge, but mainly it has been a joy. Yes, it has even been "fun." And…I no longer regret that God gave me my parents. I delight that God had so much love, so much grace and so much wisdom, both for them and for me, that He gave us to one another.

Endnotes

[i] Romans 12:6 Having then gifts differing according to the grace that is given to us, whether prophecy, *let us prophesy* according to the proportion of faith;

[ii] 2 Corinthians 3:17 Now the Lord is that Spirit: and where the Spirit of the Lord *is,* there *is* liberty.

[iii] Liberalism is a post-modern way of thinking. It includes, but is not limited to the belief that: the scriptures are not divinely inspired, scriptures may or may not be true, and that Jesus is not the only way to the Father. Liberalism believes that there are many roads to God; therefore it embraces Buddhism, Hinduism, Christianity, Islam, Chrislam a Christian Islam combination, or any other religion. Liberals within the Episcopal Church also believe that a variety of sexual orientations are acceptable.

[iv] 1 Corinthians 1:27-29 But God has chosen the foolish things of the world to confound the wise; and God has chosen the weak things of the world to confound the things which are mighty; And base things of the world, and things which are despised, has God chosen, *yea,* and things which are not, to bring to nothing things that are: That no flesh should glory in his presence.

[v] Matthew 16:18 And I say also unto thee, that thou art Peter, and upon this rock I will build my church; and the gates of hell shall not prevail against it.

[vi] Ten percent of your income

[vii] Psalm 46:10   Be still, and know that I *am* God: I will be exalted among the heathen; I will be exalted in the earth.

[viii] Revelation 3:20 Behold, I stand at the door, and knock: if any man hear my voice, and open the door, I will come in to him, and will sup with him, and he with me.

[ix] John 5:19 Then answered Jesus and said unto them, Honestly, I say unto you, The Son can do nothing of himself, but what he sees the Father do: those things the Son does likewise.

[x] 1 Corinthians 3:11-13 According to the grace of God which is given unto me, as a wise master-builder, I have laid the foundation, and another builds on it. But let every man be careful how he builds. For Jesus is the only foundation. Now if any man build upon this foundation gold, silver, precious stones, wood, hay, stubble; Every man's work shall be made manifest: for the day shall declare it, because it shall be revealed by fire; and the fire shall try every man's work of what it is.

[xi] Isaiah 61:3 To appoint unto them that mourn in Zion, to give unto them beauty for ashes, the oil of joy for mourning, the garment of praise for the spirit of heaviness; that they might be called trees of righteousness, the planting of the LORD, that he might be glorified.

[xii] Luke 7:47 Jesus said, "Her sins, which are many, are forgiven; therefore she loves much: if someone is forgiven a little, they love a little."

About the Author

Joy Gartman was lost, but Jesus found her, redeemed her and gave her a new identity and purpose. She is the founder and director of World Outreach since 1985. Joy is an intercessor, author, speaker and revivalist. She has four children: Tracy, Shaun, David and Dru.

Paperback Books available:
World Outreach
P.O. Box 417893
Sacramento CA 95841
email joygartman@gmail.com

Special Prices offered only through World Outreach include shipping and handling.
WHITE TRASH mini-book 5.00
WHITE TRASH REDEEMED Life Edition 8.00
Special limited time offer for witnessing: White Trash mini-book, 25 or more books at 2.50 each, includes shipping.

Available 1/1/13
END OF THE AGE: THE BOOK OF REVELATION Study Guide 10.00

E Books available on line at Amazon (Kindle) and Barnes and Noble (Nook).